People From My Neighbourhood

Also by Hiromi Kawakami from Granta Books

Strange Weather in Tokyo
The Nakano Thrift Shop
The Ten Loves of Mr Nishino

People From My Neighbourhood

Hiromi Kawakami

Translated from the Japanese by Ted Goossen

GRANTA

Granta Publications, 12 Addison Avenue, London W11 4QR

First published in Great Britain by Granta Books, 2020

All the stories in this volume originally appeared in the Japanese literary magazine *Monkey* or its predecessor, *Monkey Business*, edited by Motoyuki Shibata 柴田元幸 and published by Switch Publishing. Twenty-six of them were published by Switch Library (スイッチ　パブリッシング) in Japan in 2016 in the book *Kono atari no hitotachi* (このあたりの人たち). The following ten stories were not in that book, and appeared subsquently in *Monkey* (the number refers to the issue of the magazine): 'Eye Medicine', M 9; 'Weightlessness', M 10; 'Hair', M 12; 'Baby', M 13; 'The Family Trade', M 14; 'The Bottomless Swamp', M 15; 'Falsification', M 18; 'Refrigerator', M 16; 'Shack', M 17; 'The Empress', M 11.

A CIP catalogue record for this book is available from the British Library

9 8 7 6 5 4 3 2

ISBN 978 1 84627 698 9
eISBN 978 1 84627 700 9

www.granta.com

Typeset by Avon DataSet, 4 Arden Court, Alcester, Warwickshire

Printed and bound by CPI Group (UK) Ltd, Croydon, CR0 4YY

Contents

The Secret

A white cloth was lying at the foot of a zelkova tree. When I walked over and picked it up, I saw a child underneath.

'What's the big idea?' The child glared up at me.

It had narrow eyes but thick eyebrows. I couldn't tell if it was a girl or a boy.

'Oops. Sorry!' I apologized. But the child kept glaring at me. 'Are you playing hide-and-seek or something?' It shook its head vigorously from side to side.

'I live here,' it said.

The cloth was big enough to carry things in if you folded it at the corners. Tall grass twisted and curled around the child's legs.

I took a step back and turned to leave. I could feel the child's eyes on my back as I walked away. The hair on its body was thick and downy.

The following day the same cloth was lying under the zelkova tree. Damned if I'll pick it up this time, I thought, but just then the child sprang up in front of me.

'Let's go!' it sang out, and headed down the road. I didn't intend to follow, but it was taking the path that I had to walk to get back to my room, so naturally I tagged along.

The child went straight to my door. 'Open it,' it said. Its tone was so bossy I couldn't say no. The child and I entered together. The room became its home.

Luckily for me, it didn't eat very much. And it was an unexpectedly good listener. It would listen to my tales of woe – my failures at work, my diffident lover – with great sympathy, nodding as I spoke.

The child was always excited after a shower. It would dance madly around the room naked, its little penis bobbing up and down. It appeared to be a boy after all.

Sometimes, the boy would disappear for no apparent reason. After he'd been gone for a week or so, I would go back to the zelkova and find him sleeping under the white cloth.

'Why did you leave?' I'd ask.

'I don't know,' he'd answer.

I began to doubt he was a human child. It didn't matter to me, though.

He's been with me now for thirty years.

He hasn't changed in all that time. He continues to eat sparingly and to be a great listener. He still dances his funny dance after his shower, and he still disappears from time to time.

I've come to realize that he can't be human after all, seeing how he's stayed the same all these years.

Humans change over time.

I certainly have. I've aged and become grumpy. But I've come to love him, though I didn't at first. I bought a flat. And a dog. And three cats. I developed a fear of death.

The dog died, and the cats too. Now only the child and I remain. Before too long, he'll be the only one left.

'Why did you come here?' I asked him once.

He thought for a moment.

'It's a secret,' he said at last.

Chicken Hell

There's a hell, the old man said, for people who are mean to chickens. If you get sent there, a giant chicken comes and spits fire on you, and pecks you, and tramples you with its claws. And that goes on for ever.

I listened. The old man was a member of what had been the biggest farming family in our area. Now they were farmers in name only – they had sold almost all their land, and blocks of flats and housing estates stood on what had once been their fields. The old man still raised goats and chickens in his yard, but no one from the main branch of the family had anything to do with agriculture. The young people all commuted to white-collar jobs in the centre of Tokyo, in business districts like Shinbashi and Shinagawa.

He was raising about ten chickens. Some were fine cockerels with magnificent combs; others looked worn out and bedraggled.

'The strong ones peck the weak ones,' he told me. I was dying to see the weak ones get pecked, but it never seemed to happen when I was there, no matter how closely I watched. Instead, each chicken wandered around the yard by itself, quite unconcerned as to whether another chicken happened to be nearby or not.

The old man was missing an eye. 'Lost it in the war,' he said. In its place he wore a glass eye that never moved. Sometimes he'd take it out and show it to me. It was cloudy white, and bigger than the biggest marble I'd ever seen.

'Lookee here!' he'd say, thrusting it at me in his right palm. He knew it scared me.

Not long ago I went to a big art museum and saw a painting of *Chicken Hell*. And all that time, I thought he had made it up! An illustration in a thirteenth-century Kamakura hand scroll. A national treasure. It showed a scaly breasted giant cockerel with both wings extended.

The old man sometimes tormented his own chickens. When he put feed out in their box they'd all come running. Then he'd kick them away. If he was in a particularly black mood, he'd chase them around the yard.

His chickens laid lots of eggs, which he piled up in a bamboo basket. I never got a single one, however longingly I looked at them. When a hen stopped laying, the old man always let it live. 'Can't stand breaking their necks,' he said.

I once witnessed him bury a dead chicken in the backyard. 'Why don't you eat it?' I asked. 'Won't eat 'em if they die of natural causes,' he replied.

I haven't a clue what he is doing these days. I stopped visiting him around the time I entered the fourth grade, and that was that. A small white building stands where his house used to be; its ground floor is occupied by an antique shop and a patisserie. Their Mont Blanc cake is delicious.

Grandma

I can't remember her name. 'Grandma' was what I called her, but, looking back, she must have been in her mid-forties at the time. I would drop by her place every two or three days on my way home from elementary school. It was so much more fun playing with her than with my school friends. My friends were barbarians.

Grandma was always by herself. She told me she was just looking after the house, so I should come on in. It was a big house. I glimpsed a little boy younger than me on several occasions, but he always ran away and hid somewhere in the back, so I never met him. Grandma's room had a *kotatsu* table, brightly coloured origami paper, a pack of Japanese *hanafuda* cards, and her tea things: a large Thermos, a teapot, teacups and a container of green tea.

We always played cards. Since *hanafuda* is usually played with three people, we quickly ran out of cards in our hands and played off the table. As a result, we amassed all kinds of bonuses that would have been virtually impossible had there been three of us: sets of four and even five 'lights', for example, and triple red and blue 'month' combinations.

Every so often, Grandma would ask me for money. 'Ten yen, please,' she would say. I didn't have it the first time, but the next time she asked I was prepared. She praised me that one time, but after that she seemed to take the money for granted, though I handed it to her with immense pride.

Grandma was subject to terrible moods. She would sit there sullenly, folding the same origami figure over and over again: a gaudy Fukusuke, the big-headed dwarf, for example, clad in *hakama* made from equally gaudy paper of a different design and a glittering *kamishimo* ceremonial jacket. Then she would toss the whole lot into the corner.

I was introduced to the word 'hell' in her room.

'I've been told hell smells like cod liver oil,' she announced one day. Cod liver oil was provided in the school nurse's room during our lunch break, but only children whose parents had registered and paid got it. I said I wanted some too, but my mother called it a 'waste of money', and rejected the idea out of hand. When Shimizu and Kanae came back from their visit to the nurse, they said it tasted yucky and I was lucky not to get it.

'Does it smell bad?' I asked Grandma.

'It stinks,' she replied.

Then I'm glad I don't have to drink it, I thought.

She had recently changed her hairstyle. The fringe now jutted weirdly over her face like the eaves of a house, while a mini-chignon covered the nape of her neck. When I asked, 'Can I touch the front?' she glared at me. Not long after that my visits stopped. 'Let's play,' I would call from outside her window, but she would just slide it open a crack, poke her nose out and say, 'No,' in a cold, dismissive tone.

Grandma went into hospital. I guessed she was dying, but she was allowed to return home after a while. I started visiting her again, but I was a third-grader by then, so I didn't go very often. 'Did they make you drink cod liver oil in the hospital?' I asked, but she just shook her head. 'My illness isn't that simple,' she said in a patronizing tone. She was hospitalized twice more, and discharged both times. After that, she suddenly became a normal old woman, pottering about in her garden, sweeping the road in front of her house and fussing over the neighbourhood children.

The Office

He called it his office, but it was really just a gazebo in the park.

Although he rarely attended school, he always wore school uniform. It was so old the black had faded to a dull purplish hue. If you got close, you'd catch a whiff of mothballs.

He was not a big talker. He had three set phrases – 'Shall I sign here?' 'Final balance, please' and 'It's raining hard today' – and that was it.

He would take a cushion and a writing pad with him when he went to his office. Then he would sit there drawing on the pad with a pencil stub.

The cushion wasn't for him – he sat cross-legged on the gazebo bench. Rather, it was for guests. If someone approached him, he would turn the cushion over and push it in their direction. I was afraid to talk to him alone, so I always got Kanae to go with me.

Kanae was pretty nasty. She would boss him around, commanding him to recite the two times table and so forth. 'Shall I sign here?' he would mumble and fall silent.

I went to see him by myself only twice. The first time was the day we heard that a big typhoon was about to hit. I got worried and went to check on him, but he wasn't there. The second time was not long after that, when I took him a deep-fried bun left over from my school lunch. I placed it on his knee but he pushed it away. 'Final balance, please,' he said. I was upset – I had saved it especially for him – so I stamped my foot. He looked startled. Then he squeezed his eyes tight shut and clamped his hands over his ears.

I didn't find out he was four years older than I was until I started junior high. By then he had stopped going to the office. Sometimes we would bump into each other on the street. I would say hello, and he would say, 'Shall I sign here?' 'All right,' I would answer, and he would continue, 'Final balance, please.' Then, whether I nodded yes or shook my head no, he would walk away.

He had an exhibition of his drawings at the children's centre, so I went with Kanae. He had drawn pictures of animals, boats, flowers, and so forth in crayon on sheets of drawing paper. I couldn't judge their quality, but I still found them amazing.

He made a bit of a name for himself, appearing on TV from time to time. He got rid of the school uniform and started wearing striped shirts and overalls. When we met on the street he would still ask, 'Shall I sign here?' Once I didn't answer but just stood there, looking at him. 'Deep-fried buns are yummy,' he said. It was the first time I heard him say anything other than his three phrases. Then he walked away without waiting for my reply.

He died at thirty-three. A collection of his drawings was published posthumously and apparently sold very well. I leafed through it in a bookshop, but the illustrations seemed terribly flat compared to the actual drawings I'd seen at the children's centre.

Brains

Kanae had an older sister.

Her hair was straight and long, and her eyes had a hint of blue. Although the colour was like a Westerner's, her flat face was Japanese, no question.

'That's not my sister, that's a stranger,' Kanae would say from time to time. Kanae was a mean kid. Although two years her senior, her sister was clearly the one who was intimidated.

Kanae's house had two floors. The kitchen and living room were on the ground floor, the girls' room and their parents' bedroom on the first. The parents' bedroom had a double bed, still quite a rarity at that time. I always looked forward to sneaking into the room with Kanae and jumping on it.

One day, we were in there bouncing wildly in the air when we noticed Kanae's sister standing in the doorway, watching us.

'Tell Mum and you'll be sorry,' Kanae threatened. Her sister spun about and ran down the stairs. Not long after, their mother came stomping up from below and flung open the door. By that time, of course, Kanae and I were no longer jumping on the bed. Instead, we were sitting beside it, our faces the picture of innocence, pretending to play with our dolls. We'd rushed to Kanae's room to get them the moment we'd heard her mother's footsteps on the stairs.

Expelled from the bedroom, we moved to the girls' room, where we found Kanae's sister. 'You asked for it!' Kanae said, and began tickling her. I tickled her too. It seemed like harmless fun at first, but as we kept it up her sister started acting strange. Her spasms of laughter turned into strangled cries that hovered halfway between sobs and hiccups.

When at last we stopped, Kanae's sister was face down on the floor. 'She can't stand being tickled,' Kanae said lightly, pulling her over on to her back. A narrow stream of saliva trickled from her sister's mouth. I was relieved to see that she was breathing and her bluish eyes were open. They were wet with tears.

Not long after that, I visited Kanae's house again. She was out playing somewhere – only her sister was at home. 'Want to come in?' she asked. I found it somehow impossible to refuse.

She took me to their room, opened the desk drawer, and pulled out a small box. She snapped open the lid. Inside was a whitish, squishy substance. I asked her what it was. 'Brains,' she replied. 'Doll brains. They're from Tammy, the one lying over there on the shelf.'

She was pointing to the yellow-haired doll Kanae had pretended to be playing with in her parents' bedroom the last time I was there. 'You're a liar,' I shot back, but Kanae's sister just gave a faint smile.

I ran down the stairs and out into the street. My shoes were only half on, but I rushed along anyway. When one fell off, I frantically stuck my foot back in and kept running. Doll brains looked dark and somehow unclean around the edges – they weren't pure white at all.

The Crooner

Blackie was vicious.

Blackie was the name we gave the black dog that belonged to Kiyoshi Akai. He called the dog John, but there was nothing John-like about it. No, a common black Japanese mutt like that could only be called Blackie.

Blackie was a barker. Not only did he bark, he bit – and not playful little nips either. His bites were serious, the kind that draw blood. We often saw his victims in front of the Akais' house, complaining. 'Look at the blood!' they'd bellow. 'What are you going to do about it?' Yet the boy and his mother always appeared quite unperturbed.

Blackie was allowed to run free until sunset. He would go from house to house in the neighbourhood, as if patrolling his territory, thrusting his muzzle into the hedges and sniffing furiously. If you crossed his path, he would bark like crazy, and if you tried to run, he would chase you until he caught you. Then he would bite.

Of course we all detested Blackie. If a much larger dog started barking at him, we egged the larger dog on. Blackie's response was to bark a few times and then make a quick exit, tail between his legs. 'Serves you right!' everyone would shout. But there were few big dogs around, so Blackie was usually king of his domain.

The plot to kill Blackie was hatched by my friend Shimizu's older brother and his pals. Their idea was to poison him with pieces of meat laced with washing powder. They chose to do it in the daytime, when he was out and about, and successfully fed him the meat. But though he gobbled up every last bit, he remained healthy. The washing powder didn't faze him at all.

Blackie caught a thief. We heard him barking with all his might at a burglary taking place just two houses down from Kanae's place. When the startled thief tried to flee, Blackie bit him. Usually he would bite and let go, but this time he hung on to the thief's leg for all he was worth. Apparently the thief started to cry. It hurts, it hurts, he kept whimpering through his tears.

Shimizu's older brother and his buddies dismissed the thief as 'a loser'. Nevertheless, from that point on, they gave up trying to poison Blackie.

Blackie died three years later. A dumper truck hit him on the main road. Kiyoshi dug a grave for him in the garden with an angry look on his face. Nobody liked Kiyoshi either, but when this happened we felt some sympathy for him. That sympathy soon evaporated, however, when he built a weird-looking statue next to the grave.

The statue was made of Plasticine and seemed to have been modelled on Blackie. Yet Kiyoshi was no artist, so it was quite misshapen and didn't really resemble Blackie at all. Exposed to the wind and the rain, it soon began to fall apart. Kiyoshi would pick up the broken pieces and stick them back on, so that the statue came to look less and less like Blackie.

The Akais moved away not long after that. There was a rumour that Kiyoshi grew up to be a very handsome man who made the rounds of nightclubs crooning old-fashioned Japanese songs, but I have no idea whether that rumour was true or not.

The School Principal

A school principal lived in our neighbourhood.

A dog school principal, that is.

There was a small dirt run in the park where everybody took their dogs. The people would walk in circles around the run while their pets zigzagged back and forth as the spirit moved them.

Whenever the school principal caught a dog pooing on the ground or barking at someone, he would trot over to give them a scolding.

He wore a T-shirt with the words DOG SCHOOL on the back. Across his belly was the word principal. I would say he was in his fifties. He spent pretty much every weekday at the dog run.

The school principal was as bald as an egg. When a child called him 'baldie', he would smile and pat him or her on the head. But his eyes weren't smiling.

I talked to the school principal on several occasions. He always initiated the conversation, though, not me. Whenever I took my dog to the run, he'd greet me with a bow, and I would have no choice but to bow back. He would come up to me and say, 'That's a mixed breed, isn't it?' When I gave a noncommittal nod, he would go on, 'Marvellous. They're a heck of a lot better than those expensive pedigree dogs they sell in pet shops. Give me a mutt any time.'

I would give a faint nod and escape. I wanted nothing to do with him. I thought he wouldn't approach me if I wasn't with my dog, so I began going for a walk by myself. The first few times, he left me alone, but finally he had to ask.

'Where's your dog?' he said. 'Is he sick or something?' I shook my head, but from then on I couldn't avoid him.

The school principal had a way with dogs – all he had to do was click his tongue to make them obey. Apparently, some people paid him to train their dogs. 'It's not cheap, though,' he said. 'After all, it's a private school we're running.'

One time I brought up the story of Blackie, the dog that went around biting people in the neighbourhood back when I was a kid.

'Oh, yes,' he replied. 'I know all about him. Belonged to the Akais, if I'm not mistaken.'

When I expressed my surprise, the school principal introduced himself by name. It turned out that he and I had been attending the same elementary school around the time Blackie was alive.

The principal still hated his class teacher. Said she'd made him stand in the school corridor for three hours straight. His crime was stuffing a girl's satchel full of chicken bones he'd carefully collected for her.

'Why would you do something like that?' I asked.

'Every time I ate roast chicken, I licked all the bones clean and kept them for her,' he proclaimed. 'How could that be seen as anything other than an act of love?'

The school principal had a wife and two daughters. His wife was a lawyer and his daughters both worked in banks.

'They lead such boring lives.' He laughed, but his eyes weren't laughing.

Occasionally, the school principal wore a wig to the park. It was chestnut brown and parted on the side.

The Love

The middle-aged woman who ran the Love, a tiny drinking place, had the face of a demon.

She didn't scream at people or scold the neighbourhood children. Although her face was the spitting image of the demons you see in old paintings, her personality was actually quite pleasant.

The Love opened at seven-thirty in the morning. Its breakfast special cost three hundred yen. For that you would get two rolls and an iced coffee. Since the coffee came in cartons from the supermarket, it was always iced, summer and winter.

Lunch began at noon. There were two set meals on the menu: the Hamburger Special and the Meat Bun Special. Both were ready meals and came in vacuum-packed bags, so they tasted exactly the same; the only difference was their shape.

The nights were for karaoke. Few customers ever came. So the woman usually just sang by herself. Since she left the door open, we could hear her clearly on the street. When the night was young, she would sing 'Francine's Song', but when it got late, she would switch to 'White Butterfly Samba' and 'Hardly Worth Confessing'.

The Love closed at 11 p.m. Since the woman got up shortly before seven-thirty and went to bed just after eleven, her working hours matched her private time. In fact, the Love and her home were one and the same. When she shut up shop, she simply washed her hair in the sink and scrubbed her body with a well-wrung-out towel. Then she spread her mattress on the raised tatami platform where her supposed customers sat. There were no rooms at the back. The space on both sides of the counter, the raised tatami platform, the toilet, the sink – that was the whole shebang.

The woman's private possessions – clothes, make-up, photo albums, and so on – were packed in a semi-transparent plastic box kept on a corner of the raised platform. On those rare occasions when more space was needed and the platform was in use, someone would have to sit on the box.

The woman had a daughter. Sometimes the daughter returned to the Love, her old home, to spend the night. Her mother would have her sleep on the raised platform and spread a straw mat under the counter stools for herself.

'How could I let my young daughter sleep on concrete?' she'd say. 'Girls her age need to keep warm.'

Not long ago, the menu of the Love expanded. Before, the woman basically served everyone the leftovers of what she herself was eating for breakfast, lunch and dinner. Sometimes, when she tired of hamburgers, meat buns and bread rolls, for a short while she would shift to curry, *shumai* dumplings (both vacuum-packed, of course), and melon rolls. As a rule, though, the menu was hamburgers, meat buns and bread rolls, whatever the season.

The new, expanded menu includes stewed squash, rice porridge and chopped spinach. The woman's daughter has a child now, you see, and these are the foods the baby is being weaned on. It goes without saying that the woman buys them vacuum-packed, and that what the sign in the Love trumpets as 'Brand New Dishes' are essentially leftovers, too.

No one from our neighbourhood ever enters the Love. When customers do wander in, they come rushing out a few moments later. How the woman ever makes a living running that place is a mystery to us all.

The Juvenile Delinquent

Kanae turned into a juvenile delinquent.

No sooner had we entered junior high school than she began sporting long skirts that reached her ankles, a satchel squished flat as a pancake, and hair so bleached it was the colour of an ear of corn.

The first year, she'd still respond when I greeted her on the street, but by the second year we were like total strangers. By then, she was attended by a circle of admirers, girls with skirts as long as hers and boys whose hair was stiff with gel. Kanae had become the 'woman' of the 'boss' of our local teenage biker gang.

Every evening, a motorcycle would come to Kanae's house. The thought that the boss had come to pick her up excited me, but when I ran over to check him out, I found I was mistaken. A boss, it seems, never stoops to collect his own woman.

Kanae straddled the back of the bike, her face blank, arms wrapped around the waist of the driver, a huge, powerfully built high-school student. Her corn-coloured hair fluttered in the breeze. Not long after that, I heard that same student and the boss had fought a duel to the death over her. The word *duel* amazed me.

Eventually, the boss was arrested by the cops. There was a spectacular street battle between gangs, and one gang member was killed. A girl in my class told me that the boss had been shipped off to the Nerima Youth Detention Centre.

When a new boss replaced the old one, the circle around Kanae shrank. By our third year of junior high, no one was left, and Kanae had taken to dyeing her hair black. I thought that might mean she'd go back to being the same old Kanae and start studying for the high school entrance exams, but instead it seems that she replaced her gang activities with 'impure relations with the opposite sex'.

That, at least, is what I was told by one of the neighbourhood women. According to her, Kanae would go up to the roof of the school each night around ten o'clock to engage in impure relations with a succession of boys. 'It's Soeda and Fukushima and Shimizu and more besides,' the woman whispered in my ear. 'They're all itching for night to fall so they can return to the roof.' I was amazed she knew all their names, even though she didn't have a school-age child of her own.

Kanae's bad reputation continued to spread until the day of her graduation. She attended a private high school far from the neighbourhood, went on from there to vocational school, and then became a fashion designer. 'She's gone to France to study,' one of the local women told me. Not the same one who listed the boys with whom Kanae had engaged in impure relations.

Kanae's hair was pink when she returned from France. Her photograph began to appear in magazines. In her thirties, she had her own brand, and her hair had turned from pink to green to gold to white. When

I bumped into one of the neighbourhood women, she praised Kanae to the skies as 'the pride of our hometown'. It was the very same woman who had told me about Kanae's impure relations. I was amazed at her use of the word 'hometown'.

The Tenement

The tenement was home to an old taxi driver. The building looked ancient – the old man liked to boast it had been built before the Meiji Restoration of 1868. It was a total wreck, and he was the only person living there. The tenement consisted of a terrace of four houses: the taxi driver lived in the one on the far left, while his taxi occupied the one on the far right, which had been stripped of its floor and walls.

The old man didn't work much. In fact, he took his taxi out just two days a week. He'd leave around noon and be back by evening.

Once a year, the old man would leave his house for three days straight. That was in mid-January, the period that used to be called the second New Year. He would wake up the morning of his departure and prepare a dozen rice balls. Then he would fill a big Thermos with tea, and pack six boiled eggs and six mandarin oranges.

The old man would set off around noon, a satchel full of food on the seat beside him. The first afternoon was spent driving all around the neighbourhood. Our district was so small he could have covered every street in less than half an hour, but the old man stopped to rest at each park or local shrine he passed, and sat in his car for close to an hour near the main shopping area, so that by the time he had completed his route, the day was already over.

Although the old man was presumably alone all that time, strangely the rice balls, boiled eggs and mandarin oranges had somehow disappeared when he'd finished his round. The old man hadn't eaten them. We knew that because, as was his custom, he went on to the noodle restaurant Ramen Five in the centre of town for their ramen-and-fried-rice special.

When night fell, the old man drove to the Chūō Expressway. Where he went from there was anybody's guess. We heard that someone had seen him exiting the expressway near Kōfu to head into the mountains, but that was just rumour.

'Where do you disappear to, anyway?' the woman who runs the Love, the small local drinking place, finally asked him.

'I go driving with the girls,' he replied.

'The girls' were the women he claimed inhabited the empty houses in the tenement. There were three, all of whom had died in the years before the Restoration.

'You mean they're ghosts?'

'Ha-ha-ha. Yep, you could say that, but women are women. They're still fun to have around, even if they look sort of blurry and don't have legs.'

Having three must be a problem sometimes, the woman from the Love teased. The old man guffawed.

Not long ago I went down to the town hall to check their registry. The tenement had been built just after the Second World War, it turned out, and the records showed no one presently residing there.

Yet the old man is still living in the tenement. 'Aren't you a ghost yourself?' the woman from the Love asked him, but he just laughed. Then he went down to Ramen Five and polished off their ramen-and-fried-rice special, with side orders of Chinese chive dumplings and pickled bamboo shoots, in the twinkling of an eye.

The Hachirō Lottery

My family lost the Hachirō lottery. Twice.

The first time was when I was four years old, the second when I was in the third grade.

The lottery loser was determined by a random draw. That meant there were some families that never lost, and other unlucky families that lost a number of times. The worst case was the Kawamata family two doors down from Kanae's, who lost the lottery on eleven separate occasions.

Each loss was good for three months. Hachirō would live in your home during that time, and it was your family's responsibility to feed him and make sure he attended school regularly. You were allowed to ask him to perform normal chores but not to keep him home from school to work, nor to demand that he run errands late at night. He was also to be paid an allowance.

Hachirō was a big eater, whose presence caused a family's food bills to shoot through the roof. He was a troublemaker, too, which meant those looking after him were often called in for teachers' meetings, after which they had to write formal letters to apologize for whatever rules he had broken.

Hachirō always had a ready tongue.

If you said anything at all critical to him he

flared up – talking back, griping, even making false accusations. For example, not long after the family that ran Ramen Five, the noodle restaurant, lost the lottery, dumplings temporarily disappeared from the menu. Hachirō's constant complaints about how horrid they were had driven the owner around the bend.

Hachirō was the fifteenth child born to a family called Shikishima. They had seven girls and eight boys, of whom Hachirō – literally 'number eight' – was the youngest. It was because the Shikishimas were unable to look after so many children that it was decided that Hachirō should rotate among the families in the neighbourhood.

I've been listing Hachirō's defects, but he had his good points, too.

For one thing, he had green fingers when it came to growing herbs; for another, he had a gift for a certain kind of sculpture.

Huge clumps of mallow, savory, borage, peppermint willow and other exotic herbs, planted and tended by Hachirō's own hands, filled the gardens of all the houses he had lived in. Since no one knew how to cook with them, though, they were left to go wild.

As for sculpture, well, Hachirō was able to turn out exquisitely detailed models of the human heart. This was apparently a Shikishima family tradition. They looked so gross that people kept them out of sight.

The second time Hachirō stayed in our home he was in junior high. He was a terrible pain in the neck, peeking at me whenever I took a bath and pestering me, a mere third-grader, to help him with his homework, but every once in a while we'd meet outside the house and he'd treat me to ice cream.

Hachirō kept rotating among the families in our neighbourhood until he finished junior high, at which point the Hachirō lottery came to an end. He continued his studies at night school and worked for a construction company during the day. After graduating from university, he got an architect's license and set up his own business, then offered to renovate or rebuild many of the houses he had stayed in at a special, very low price.

You could always tell which families had taken Hachirō up on his offer. The giveaway was that somewhere on their walls or fence there would be a heart sculpted in realistic detail. Families turned off by this idea would avoid him, however cheap his price. This so infuriated Hachirō that he began sneaking into their gardens to plant large quantities of flea-killing chrysanthemum. Apart from its insecticidal properties, this plant is known for its terrible stench.

The Magic Spell

The Kawamata family came back from America.

The father and mother had headed off to America immediately after they were married to spend ten years running a business in California, then they shut up shop and returned to Japan with a hefty chunk of foreign currency.

'And they got to know some Hollywood stars, too!' one of the neighbourhood women gushed.

As you might expect, their daughters were thoroughly American. Dolly was the elder, and Romi the younger. Dolly was five and Romi two, and they sported matching lace-up shoes.

Kanae was fascinated by the whole Kawamata family.

'Let's go and pick on Dolly,' she said to me. 'Let's show her how mean Japanese kids can be.' So off we went to the park where Dolly was playing.

Dolly had built a mountain in the sandpit and was busy digging a tunnel through the base of it.

'You're going to get it now, Dolly!' Kanae jeered. But Dolly kept working on the tunnel as if she wasn't there.

When we took a closer look, we saw that the mountain was much more polished than what a child would normally build. The peak was firmly packed, and the sides sloped gently towards the bottom in a leisurely arc. Even the tunnel wasn't a simple hole but a deftly shaped horseshoe.

Kanae and I stood there lost in admiration, our plan to torment Dolly forgotten.

Dolly was painstaking in her work. She'd dig out a little sand, toss it away, and pat the sides of the mountain to firm it up. Then she'd scrape out more sand and throw it away. Now and then, though, a small part of the tunnel would collapse, and Dolly would cry out, 'Oops!'

Kanae and I were amazed – we'd never heard the word 'oops' before.

'What did she say?'

'Maybe it's a magic spell.'

Dolly patiently completed the repairs, then returned to her digging. But the tunnel suffered another partial collapse.

'Oops!' she cried again. We jumped out of our skins. By the end of the day, she had uttered 'Oops!' a total of twenty times.

Dolly was still digging when Kanae and I visited the park the next day. This time there were seventeen 'Oops!' There were nine the following day, but the day after that was Sunday, so we didn't go to the park.

From then on, Kanae and I took to chanting 'Oops!' when we buried treasure or placed a curse on someone.

The Kawamatas eventually settled into the neighbourhood. Before long Dolly and Romi's mother was calling them Midori and Hiromi, and no one could tell they'd once lived in America; yet Kanae and I continued to intone 'Oops!' whenever the need arose.

The very last time we used it was in third grade. 'Make our breasts big!' we implored, then solemnly chanted 'Oops!' twenty times each. Kanae and I wanted to grow breasts as quickly as possible so that we could fight aliens, wicked religious sects, and other forces of evil.

Grandpa Shadows

Grandpa Shadows lived on the outskirts of town. His home was a mansion that had fallen into disrepair. Two banana trees and a riot of sago palms dominated his garden. I was told by the old chicken farmer who lived in the neighbourhood that in bygone days, the garden had been beautifully tended and carpeted with grass.

We called him Grandpa Shadows because he had two shadows.

One shadow was docile and submissive, the other rebellious. The rebellious one was always pushing the docile one around or running off somewhere or behaving in a manner that bore no relationship to what Grandpa Shadows was doing. On occasion, it would even attach itself to another person and refuse to leave for two or three days. The time it latched on to Kiyoshi Akai was the worst. Since the shadow belonged to a very old man, it tired easily, so when Kiyoshi started running, it began to gasp and wheeze in a most theatrical way. Then it verbally attacked him.

'The damned thing's always threatening me,' Kiyoshi grumbled. 'Accuses me of trying to kill it, says it'll send me to hell.'

It was Hachirō who told me Grandpa Shadows had once been a baron, a member of the pre-war nobility. He had hosted balls in his mansion: lords squiring ladies in evening gowns would arrive in horse-drawn carriages night after night.

'So did you ever see a horse-drawn carriage?' I asked the chicken man. He just let out a big burp.

Rumour had it that Grandpa Shadows had already passed away. Otherwise how could he have two shadows? It was also said that whomever the shadow attached itself to died within ten days.

But Kiyoshi didn't die. Instead, he and his vicious dog, Blackie, continued their reign of terror in the neighbourhood.

One time, however, Kiyoshi did come close to death. He was struck by a car and lay unconscious for a full week. We all shed tears for him. Although Kanae's were of the crocodile variety, Hachirō's were genuine. Kiyoshi and Hachirō had always been surprisingly close. Maybe it was because both were labelled pests by their neighbours.

'I was at Grandpa Shadows's place the whole time,' were Kiyoshi's first words when he opened his eyes. We were all amazed.

According to Kiyoshi, he had danced every night. Quadrilles and waltzes and foxtrots. So many of the gowned ladies wanted him as their dancing partner that he had a hard time shaking them off. Grandpa Shadows never danced, just sipped tall glasses of banana juice.

They tore Grandpa Shadows's mansion down several years after Kiyoshi's accident. Grandpa Shadows, who was 103 at the time, was moved to a fancy seafront nursing home. It appears that the rebellious shadow took to attaching itself to other aged residents, all of whom died soon afterwards.

The Six-Person Flats

There is a council housing estate on the outskirts of town where most of the flats have families of six.

Some families are made up of two parents, two grandparents, and two kids, while others have parents and four children, or include cousins and the like.

For some reason, families of three or four or five are rare, while families of six comprise a full ninety per cent of the estate's residents.

It was Mrs Kawamata, just back from America, who started the whispering campaign against the estate. She claimed that abroad the number six was considered 'unlucky'.

'It's the devil's number,' she would confide in hushed tones to anyone and everyone she came across in the neighbourhood.

Gradually, people from town began to avoid the housing estate. Mrs Kawamata's rumour campaign was not the only cause; there was also a string of strange events that befell those who visited the place.

Mr Sawaki's beard, for example, started growing at a startling rate: though he shaved every morning, by evening it would be a bush of at least twenty centimetres. Ms Arashimura's feet, on the other hand, developed puddles. Not water blisters, but real puddles, said to have tadpoles merrily swimming around in them. The case that grabbed me most was that of Kanae's big sister, who acquired the ability to speak in the voices of the dead. The day after she returned from her visit to the six-person flats, for example, she channelled the voices of Prince Shōtoku, Leonardo da Vinci, and Yang Guifei, wailing on and on in the most pitiful tone that the world 'had taken a wrong turn'. I found the idea so fascinating that I ran over to Kanae's as soon as I could. Say something in the comedian Kingorō Yanagiya's voice, I begged, whereupon her sister's face became a wrinkled mask that looked just like Kingorō. 'Oh, my dear lady!' was the only line I could get out of her.

We were terribly excited by this, but Kiyoshi set us straight. 'Come on,' he said, 'don't you know mediums can only communicate with the dead? Kingorō's still alive.' When I reported this news to Kanae's sister, she didn't miss a beat. 'He just died,' she said.

Once it became clear that the town would have nothing to do with it, the estate struck out on its own, erecting its own school, post office, town hall, shops, office buildings – the whole works. It even minted its own currency, with a creepy symbol of six heads clumped together.

The town grew more and more run down as time passed, but the estate thrived. It seceded from Japan and formed its own armed forces, which sometimes held manoeuvres in Tokyo Bay. Not long afterwards, the curse was broken. Mr Sawaki's beard went back to normal, and Ms Arashimura's tadpoles sprouted legs and hopped away as frogs, after which the puddles on her feet disappeared. Only Kanae's sister retained her mysterious power. Eventually, she made a name for herself as one of the mediums who speak for the dead on sacred Mount Osore, famous for her ability to channel Kingorō Yanagiya.

The Rivals

Two girls named Yōko grew up across the street from one another in our neighbourhood. One girl's name was written with the character for *sheep* – I shall call her Yōko One. The other, whom I will call Yōko Two, used the character for *enchantress* in her name.

Both attended private girls' schools, unusual in our town, where almost all the children went to the local state school.

The principal of Yōko One's school was a nun. When Yōko One bragged, 'My principal's really old, but her face is as smooth as silk,' Yōko Two was ready with a comeback. 'Big deal. My principal's whole head is smooth, right to the very top. Not a wrinkle anywhere.' Her principal, you see, was a Buddhist priest.

The two girls were in constant competition with their outfits. If Yōko One flaunted the legs she was so proud of in the current fashion of miniskirts and knee-high floppy socks, Yōko Two retaliated by strutting around in a flared maxi coat, set off by the platform ankle boots she had filched from her little brother.

Both Yōkos had been born in the same year. What's more, their birthdays, blood types, and even their faces were identical.

They were after each other non-stop from the time they began to talk. 'Stop copying me!' one would say, and the other would reply, 'You're the copycat, not me.' Sparks would fly when they passed on the street. In fact, when the news forecast hazardously dry conditions, people in the neighbourhood took turns making sure the two girls stayed away from each other, for they had once actually started a small fire in the stationery shop near the train station.

After graduating from high school, Yōko One went on to college, while Yōko Two got married. When Yōko Two's husband met Yōko One, however, he fell in love at first sight, and, before you knew it, the two were carrying on in secret. Since Yōko Two's antennae were tuned in to anything to do with Yōko One, she was able to figure out the situation right away.

The townspeople held their breath. What revenge would Yōko Two wreak on her bitter adversary? Strange to tell, however, Yōko Two remained calm. It was as if the demon that had possessed her had suddenly fallen away. She greeted Yōko One on the street with a cheerful smile and started dressing demurely, forgoing the increasingly garish colours she had worn to outdo her rival. She wore only the simplest make-up and spent her holidays in the park feeding the sparrows and munching rice balls from the basket she had brought along.

It was Yōko One who found it impossible to keep her cool. It drove her crazy —she had stolen her rival's man and yet no retaliation was forthcoming. She began slapping up posters around town announcing her affair with Yōko Two's husband and making anonymous phone calls to his office to inform his superiors of what was going on. Then she sat back and waited for the response. Since Yōko Two couldn't have cared less about her husband's infidelity, however, there was no chance of a blow-up. Finally, Yōko One, her face like a demon, went to a shrine in the dead of night to cast a curse upon her rival. Observing all the formalities, she chose the third quarter of the Hour of the Ox and used the requisite twelve-centimetre nail to post her request: that Yōko Two would die young, leaving Yōko One to marry her husband and live happily ever after.

The death curse worked. But it was Yōko One, the one who had cast the curse, who died of a sudden heart attack, not Yōko Two. The two women were so similar that the god had mistaken one for the other.

Once Yōko One was dead, Yōko Two reverted to her malicious ways. She extorted a huge amount of alimony from the man who was now her ex-husband, and used the cash to launch a company that sold organic vegetables. When the profits started rolling in, she bought two houses, two boats, and two parrots. Whenever she missed her rival, as she did on occasion, she would take it out on her secretary. 'You're such a drag,' she would snap. 'Even your make-up is so damned sensible!'

The Elf

The Music House sat right next to the park.

With its chocolate-brown walls, crimson roof tiles, and tan-coloured front door and bay window, no one had a clue what style had inspired it.

No name graced its entrance. In the summer, the garden was filled with blooming sunflowers encircled by the dark green of its many trees: camphor and locust, redwood and persimmon. Although everything was beautifully tended, no one had ever seen the master of the house in the garden, or anywhere else for that matter.

You could only visit the Music House if it was your birthday. Even then, you had to be standing in front of the entrance at three o'clock sharp for the door to open.

'So what was it like?' I asked Kanae. She batted her eyelashes two or three times.

'Oh, nothing much,' she said at last.

Kanae had turned nine the day before. And although she said it was nothing much, I noticed her restless eyes combing the area. She appeared to be afraid someone might overhear what she was saying.

About half the town seemed to have paid a visit to the Music House. Yet, although so many had been there, no one ever talked in any detail about the experience. The dog school principal called it 'enchanting'. Hachirō said it was 'far-out'. The old chicken farmer felt he had heard 'a nightingale singing', while little Dolly Kawamata said, 'It was just, like, so, oops!' Even the normally voluble Kiyoshi Akai could manage nothing better than, 'Thought I heard someone playing an old dance tune. Damn!'

Stitching all these comments together, I could only assume that some kind of music could be heard at the Music House.

'Of course there's music,' Kanae's sister said coolly. 'That's why they call it the Music House.'

'But what kind of music?'

'It depends. Everyone hears different music. The music that rules their destiny. It's no joke – music really does determine your destiny, you know.'

After that, I couldn't wait to pay a visit to the Music House. When I found out the following week that the grandchild of the woman who owned the Love was having a birthday, I borrowed the toddler and, at three o'clock sharp, was standing on the doorstep.

The door creaked open.

'I'm the babysitter!' I called out as I fearfully shepherded the child through the door. Music began to play. It was Teruhiko Saigō's corny old number, 'Flamenco by Starlight'.

We spent the next hour listening to strains of 'Flamenco by Starlight'. At that point, the child started to fuss and we had to leave the Music House. Could 'Flamenco by Starlight' really be my song of destiny? Or the child's? Or both of ours? Even now it isn't clear.

Some time later, the old farmer told me his theory that the owner of the Music House was an elf covered with fur.

'The fur is really shaggy, I've been told, twisting every which way,' he said, fiddling with his false eye.

The Buriers

An enormous quantity of love letters was found discarded outside the front door of the chicken farmer. Six cardboard boxes stuffed to the brim. 'I read a few of 'em,' the old man said, spitting on the ground, 'and they were all godawful.'

Apparently, someone had left them there in the middle of the night. The farmer had heard the chickens squawking, and when he went outside to investigate, there the boxes were, neatly stacked in three piles like shrine offerings.

'In the old days, we would have called for the buriers,' he said.

'The buriers?' I asked, puzzled.

'You know, like the grade-school club, the kids who bury things.'

When I told him I'd never heard of a club like that, he just nodded. 'Yep, they're gone now. But we used to have 'em.'

The buriers would bury almost anything, he explained. Diaries you wanted to chuck, unneeded pots and pans. Clothes that carried unpleasant associations, broken glasses.

'The only thing they wouldn't bury was raw stuff.'

'Raw stuff?'

'Like rotten taters, dead goldfish, those kinds of

things. Boy, oh, boy,' he sighed nostalgically, 'old love letters – those would've been perfect for them.'

'But are schoolkids really able to dig proper holes?' I asked.

'You know kids that age,' he replied, shrugging his shoulders. 'There might be a piece left sticking out from the hole, or maybe the rain'd wash away whatever they'd buried. But we didn't care. We just loved watching their backs as they dug, the way they threw themselves into the work.' The old man sounded pensive, unusual for him.

He described how once when a girl had jilted him, he had crept into her house and stolen her socks, then given them to the buriers.

'You mean like those guys who steal girls' panties?' I asked.

'No,' he said, 'socks and panties ain't the same at all.'

The end of the buriers came when someone revealed that they had buried raw stuff. A group of the littler kids had buried a woman's corpse at the bottom of the school grounds.

'But it wasn't raw, to tell the truth,' the old man said. They investigated and discovered the corpse was over two hundred years old. When the children found the mummified body, they thought it was either an old kite or someone's graduation art project.

The mummy was unearthed and donated to the community centre. Even today, if you visit the centre and ask to see the mummy, they will show it to you.

In the end, the boxes of love letters left in front

of the old chicken farmer's house were buried by the policeman stationed in our neighbourhood, who, it turned out, had once been a burier himself. He said he read a few before throwing them in the hole.

'My god, they were dreadful,' he said, spitting on the ground.

Rumour has it that the letters were written by the dog school principal to his wife, but now that they've been buried, there's no way to know for sure.

Banana

Uncle Red Shoes always looked worried.

His trousers as well as his shoes were invariably a bright red. Below the top of his ears, his head was shaven, while above that his hair was stiffened with gel so that it stood up in spikes.

Though his scarlet footwear never varied, the style did: sometimes he wore shoes, sometimes lace-up boots, or, depending on the season, beach sandals.

It seemed Uncle Red Shoes had not always lived in our neighbourhood.

'I heard that he used to manage a big factory in western Honshu,' said the woman who ran the Love.

That factory apparently manufactured stuffed toy bunnies. Hoping to ride the wave of popularity for Miss Huggie, the black blow-up doll, his father had launched a new stuffed toy, a soft rabbit named Mr Bunny, which did well (though not as well as Miss Huggie), and followed it in quick succession with Mr Froggie, Puppykins (which smelled like an actual dog) and finally Mr Banana, whose skin could be peeled off and stuck back on. All of them scored a hit with the buying public.

'But the factory went bankrupt after he took over, and he came here,' she continued.

Uncle Red Shoes always sang the song 'Hardly

Worth Confessing' when he visited her place, which drove her around the bend.

'I mean, that's one of my signature songs!' she said.

People thought that the reason Uncle Red Shoes was so worried might be the financial problems he was having with the dance studio he had opened five years before.

'What sort of dance does he teach there?' I asked.

'How the heck should I know? The Banana Dance, maybe?'

Whenever I passed Uncle Red Shoes on the street, something good was sure to happen the next day. Last time I picked up a five-hundred-yen coin. The time before that I won a bottle of cooking wine at a raffle held by the local shops. And the time before that I was the one who got picked up. 'Join me for a cup of tea?' the man said, and by the end he had bought me twelve packs of fried noodles and given me ten back issues of *Shōnen Jump*.

Uncle Red Shoes lived on the third floor of the dance studio. Every once in a while, he danced on the street. Raising one leg in the air, he twirled round and round. I've seen him do as many as five pirouettes.

'You know what that step is called?' Midori Kawamata asked me when we were hanging out together.

'The Banana?' I replied, but she just shot me a dirty look.

'No, that's a *grand fouetté*.'

Not long after that, the dance studio went

bankrupt. The ground floor was turned into a second location for the Love drinking establishment and the first floor rented out as office space, but Uncle Red Shoes continued to live on the second floor, where he remains to this day. I sometimes see him dancing *grand fouettés* on the street. He looks awfully worried, but his twirls are gorgeous.

Lord of the Flies

'Any gambling joints in these parts?' Sakai asked me. He had just moved into the neighbourhood.

Gambling in our area was controlled by Uncle Round, who ran an operation on the outskirts of town. His nickname came from his round belly and the round spectacles he always wore. Uncle Round's speciality was the hog and fly game. He would line up ten pigs and people would compete to guess how many flies were buzzing around each one.

'Pigs? Flies?' Sakai asked. The idea so excited him he was shaking like a leaf. Uncle Round had exceptional kinetic vision, which allowed him to discern the exact number of flies around each pig at any given time. There was a video camera they could have used, but it was seldom needed.

Sakai headed off to Uncle Round's establishment the following day. He didn't come back until very late that night.

'How'd you get on?' I asked him the next day.

He pulled out a wad of notes and waved it under my nose. It was nearly an inch thick. He asked if I would go with him, but I said no. Kanae had dragged me along with her once, and I had lost three thousand yen. I was still in high school at the time, so it really hurt.

Sakai immersed himself in the gambling scene, going to Uncle Round's every evening. He took to wearing flashy clothes, dating a chorus line of women, and buying a string of foreign cars.

Sakai won so much money that Uncle Round's operation started going downhill. Rumour had it that Sakai was cheating, but no one was able to work out exactly how.

At a certain point, Uncle Round disappeared. His successor was – no surprise here – Sakai, who wasted little time before launching a massive renovation. He added a cabaret club, a dodgy bar, an udon noodle shop, a swimming pool and more, and draped the pigs, who had been naked in Uncle Round's day, in glittering outfits made of gold and silver thread. He placed the bronze head of a pig above the entrance. It was studded with lots of tiny flies, also done in bronze.

All this grossed out the townsfolk, who gave the place a wide berth, but outsiders thronged there. Public morals suffered as a result. The lady who ran the Love, the dog school principal, Hachirō and others joined forces to demonstrate against the gambling joint, to no effect whatsoever.

One day, a rumour spread that Uncle Round was back in town. A few days after that Sakai disappeared. The gambling joint again went into decline, reverting to what it had been in the old days – a bare-bones operation with unpretentious, naked pigs.

Much later, I had an opportunity to ask Uncle Round in private what the real story was, and he gave me the unvarnished truth. He had gone to Sakai's house, looking for revenge, and had ended up stabbing him several times in the heart. At that moment, believe it or not, what we had called Sakai turned into a large swarm of flies and flew away.

'So he was the Lord of the Flies, no question. That's why I can never be charged with murdering a human,' Uncle Round said, thumping his round stomach. It is said that to this day Uncle Round keeps the bronze pig's head in his cupboard, a relic of the Lord of the Flies.

The Baseball Game

Not long ago, Kiyoshi Akai and Michio began sneaking off after school to the local community centre behind the station, their school knapsacks still on their backs. At first they said they were going there to play ping-pong, but when we had ping-pong in PE one day, they didn't even know the rules, so it was clearly a lie.

'So what the heck do you guys do at the community centre?' Kanae grilled them, but they just clammed up. Kanae grabbed me and the two of us went to the centre to find out.

They weren't there, so Kanae cased the whole place inside and out. We spotted a cat walking on top of a nearby fence. 'Shoo!' Kanae hissed, and the cat ran off. 'This way,' she said, and headed down the narrow alley that ran alongside the centre.

We had not gone far when we heard a strange beeping sound. There was a door flanked by pots of large Omoto lilies, so we opened it and peered inside. Sure enough, there were Kiyoshi and Michio, leaning over some sort of long box.

'It's the Baseball Game!' Kanae shouted. The Baseball Game was all the rage in our neighbourhood. Despite its name, it had nothing to do with baseball, but consisted of trying to flip small balls into a hole with your finger, a bit like Smart Ball. Once you began playing you couldn't stop – an expensive addiction, since ten balls cost fifty yen. School kids had no choice but to quit when their money ran out, but when adults got hooked, the results could be horrendous. A number of lives had been ruined as a result.

'What the hell – you gonna squeal on us to the teacher?' Michio yelled back, but Kiyoshi didn't even see us, for he was too deep in the game to notice.

'That's funny,' Kanae muttered. 'Kiyoshi and Michio don't have this kind of money.'

She had a point. That's when we noticed there was a tiny child standing right behind the two boys, who handed over another fifty yen every time they ran out of balls. We had never seen the kid before. 'Something fishy is going on here,' Kanae muttered again, and strode into the room.

What we had thought was a child was actually a large bird. It had five fingers instead of talons, though, and a somewhat human face. 'Scram!' Kanae screamed. It was the same voice she had used to scare away the cat, but this time it was ten times louder. The bird flew away with a whapping of wings. Kiyoshi and Michio looked at us with glassy eyes, as though they had just awoken from a dream. It turned out that every time they took fifty yen from the bird, they had to let it peck their bottoms.

'Nuts, so it's just another pervert,' Kanae spat out, quickly scooping up the fifty yen coins still left in their hands. It's not a pervert, it's a bird, I wanted to say. But Kanae looked so scary I let it pass. Kiyoshi and Michio didn't come to school for some time after that. Our teacher said it was chicken pox, but years later Kiyoshi told me their secret: their bodies had been studded with bird-shaped boils, and they had been forced to wait until the boils subsided.

Torture

Michio kept saying he wanted a bronze statue erected of himself.

'How can I make that happen?' he asked our teacher.

The teacher took his question seriously. 'Well,' he replied, 'there are two ways. If you become very famous, people might build one in your honour. Or if you become very rich, you can pay to have one put up in front of your house.'

We all made fun of Michio when he wasn't around. The only kid in our school who didn't laugh at him was Kanae's big sister.

'Not many kids have that kind of ambition these days,' she said.

'As if you weren't a kid yourself,' Kanae shot back. Kanae tried intimidating her, but instead of cowering as she usually did, her sister just shrugged her off.

Towards the end of that year we found out that Kanae's sister and Michio were plotting a revolt against the government, with an eye to having their statues erected.

Rumours started flying.

'But what does that mean, a revolt?'

'Like signing secret pacts and stuff.'

'I heard they're stockpiling bombs.'

Kanae's sister and Michio passed each day as though nothing was out of the ordinary. Our teacher had given them a word of warning, Kanae told us.

'Where are they hiding the bombs?' I asked her. But she didn't know. For once, her sister had dug in her heels and was refusing to budge, despite Kanae's threats. That really pissed Kanae off. With no proof, our teacher was powerless to act.

The government was toppled shortly after New Year. The newspapers issued an extra edition trumpeting the news in huge headlines:

NHK FALLS TO THE REVOLUTIONARY ARMY! PRESIDENT TAKEN HOSTAGE!

Martial law was declared. From morning till night NHK, the Japan Broadcasting Corporation, ran boring videos released by the revolutionaries. Kanae railed against the fact that shows like *Tips for a Healthy Life* and *Lunch for the Salaryman* had been cancelled. Could she really be watching stuff like that? It made no sense at all.

The Revolutionary Army fell in the spring. The President was released, and all returned to normal. We still didn't know what roles Michio and Kanae's sister had played in the Revolutionary Army, or even if they had been involved.

They disappeared from view shortly after the revolution was put down. Six months later, though, they returned to school. Kanae's sister had dyed her hair bright red, while Michio carried a trumpet under his arm and seemed always to be tapping out a rhythm with his toe.

Kanae grilled her sister mercilessly, but her sister remained as cool as a cucumber.

We heard from people who lived in the neighbourhood next door that the two of them had been brutally tortured.

'Was it awful?' I whispered to Michio during our morning assembly.

'Naw,' he said, shaking his head. 'It felt just wonderful, all of it.' He wouldn't tell me what exactly had felt so wonderful.

In the end, Michio never had a statue made of himself, but more than fifty years later three were erected of Kanae's sister. Not one of her statues had anything to do with the revolution, though.

Bass Fishing

A diplomat's come to town.

It was Hachirō who spread the word.

'What the hell is a diplomat?' Kanae asked, spit spraying from her mouth.

'It's like someone who can negotiate between two countries, or someone who's part of a delegation.'

But Kanae wasn't satisfied with Hachirō's answer.

'That's too vague,' she sniffed.

'But that's what they do.'

'Has anyone actually seen this guy?' she persisted.

'The old man from the tenement says he's ridden in his cab several times.'

That clinched it for Kanae. 'Then he's a fake. A real diplomat would have his own car and chauffeur.'

But the diplomat was no fake. An embassy building was erected next to the tenement and a while later a shiny black car with chauffeur was installed in the garage. A national flag with a bizarre design was hoisted over the building, and a stream of people we had never seen before began passing through its doors night after night.

The weird thing, though, was that no one had laid eyes on the diplomat. Even the cab driver in whose car he had ridden.

'No, can't say I would know him,' the old man said,

shaking his head in puzzlement. 'There was a human shape in my mirror, but that's all I can remember. His face, his clothes, his voice – nothing registered.'

Rumour had it that the diplomat's hobby was fishing. Every Sunday, he would go to the artificial lake on the edge of town, where he would catch and release a number of black bass.

'What lake?' Kiyoshi Akai exclaimed. 'Do we even have a lake in this town?'

That caused a bit of a stir. Some said there had always been one, while others insisted no lake had existed since they were born. Tempers flared, and shots were almost fired.

Shares in the town plummeted in value, and crime soared. More and more young men resisted military service, and the number of exiles increased.

Before we knew it, people had abandoned living above ground, choosing to take shelter in caves and cellars, where it was safer. Children had to risk their lives to attend school, so they seldom went, but there were so few teachers it made little difference. Gangs of youths, based on age, right down to the little kids, fought each other in turf wars that laid waste to the town. The sole business operating above ground was the Love, now frequented by shady drug dealers, who openly trafficked in heroin and speed. Perhaps the only thing that hadn't changed was the proprietress's insistence on singing 'Hardly Worth Confessing' every night on the karaoke.

Ten years passed, then twenty and more, and the

town became a ghost town. Yet the embassy continued to prosper. The bizarre flag flew from its roof, and the diplomat's chauffeured car gleamed with fresh polish.

Then suddenly one day everything returned to normal.

The town's streets were swept and clean, the schools were reopened, and the devastated citizens were returned to youth and health. The concept of shares in the town and the practice of military service were eradicated.

Subsequently, it was whispered here and there that the diplomat was an alien from outer space who had been conducting an experiment in mass hypnosis, but no one knew if that was true or not. Even today, rumour has it that the diplomat can be seen at the artificial lake every Sunday, fishing for bass. No one has gone there to confirm that.

Pigeonitis

The first case of pigeonitis popped up right after the May holidays.

The victim was a middle-aged farmer, but it took a long time for anyone to notice, so he was already in pretty bad shape when he was diagnosed. He lay there on his sickbed clucking and cooing away. A person suffering from pigeonitis sounds like a pigeon when they try to talk. In severe cases, their body also begins to take on pigeon-like characteristics. It is so contagious that most of those who look after the sick catch it themselves.

'Anyone with symptoms, no matter how minor, must be tested without delay!' A van with a loudhailer dispatched by the town hall patrolled our streets, blasting announcements. 'Children must avoid school at all costs. If you have contracted the disease, proceed directly to the isolation wing of the hospital.'

Despite these instructions, those with mild symptoms could often avoid detection just by keeping their mouths shut.

'The problem is, the food they're serving in the isolation wing is really vile,' Kiyoshi Akai lectured us. He was our self-proclaimed expert on pigeonitis, his qualification being that he had witnessed the first case up close and seen with his own eyes how the farmer's body had been transformed.

'The first thing that happens is your chest begins to stick out like a pigeon's. Then your eyes get big and round. Finally, you begin to walk like a pigeon. You start tilting forwards from the waist, and your movements get all herky-jerky,' Kiyoshi pronounced, spit flying everywhere.

We were all frightened, with one exception – Kanae's sister. 'So your chest expands and your eyes get big and round,' she murmured. 'I could live with that.'

The biggest problem with pigeonitis was that your mind became pigeon-like. It was bad enough that you laid eggs one after another, scattered your droppings everywhere, and chased after insects; what caused even more trouble was your pattern of thought.

For one thing, you lost the power to think ahead. Completely. Your only concern was what was taking place in the immediate present. Once the disease had taken hold, our town was a terrible sight for several months. Everything was an absolute shambles, no one paid any attention to being on time, and all work was put on hold. None of this, however, bothered those who had the illness. Soon, almost everyone had caught it, and people sailed blissfully through the chaos of their daily lives.

'Eat all the bugs we want! Make all the babies we can!'

Everyone was buoyed up by this mentality, and in fact the pregnancy rate during this period skyrocketed.

You could only catch pigeonitis once, which meant the whole town was immune once the outbreak had passed. After about six months, there were no new cases, and things gradually returned to normal. We all kept quiet about what had taken place during that time, so that the solidarity of our community was actually enhanced.

Only one person in town hadn't contracted the disease – Kiyoshi. He was grief-stricken. The fact he was the one among us who *should* have caught pigeonitis seemed to make it only worse.

Once people realized how sensitive he was about it, they started ribbing him. 'What small eyes you have!' they would tease. This was because, even after recovery, people who had suffered pigeonitis had those characteristic round eyes. The farmer especially liked to tell Kiyoshi how great it felt to strut around his yard gobbling up bugs, another carry-over from the disease. Kiyoshi never responded, but he did watch the man doing this out of the corner of his eye.

Sports Day

'They're going to hold Sports Day again,' Kanae told me, as if sharing a big secret.

Our school's last Sports Day had taken place three years earlier. The police department had sponsored it, which may help explain why the events had centred around the martial arts and marksmanship. Three students from our school had taken first prize: Kiyoshi Akai in the 'thirty kilos and under' class in judo, Dolly Kawamata in the 'kata' division in karate, and Kanae's sister in the grade-school air-rifle competition. Kanae's sister's surprising success – she had been shooting for less than a year – inspired the police to send a recruiter to her home, but she turned him down flat, saying her plans for the future involved becoming a medium who communicated with the dead. Her parents displayed the Walther air rifle she had used in the competition on their living-room wall: when their home was broken into the following year, and the criminals took the parents hostage, Kanae grabbed the gun and faced them down, ending the stand-off.

'You're not the only one who can handle an air rifle,' Kanae had boasted triumphantly to her sister. That's when we realized how envious she had been. Her sister, by the way, had at the time been cloistered in the mountains with a group of budding spirit mediums at a kind of training camp.

The sponsor this time around was the local Marunaka Bank. Their plan was to open their doors and hold the events on their premises. These would include competitions for best loan evaluation, best anti-fraud strategy for direct deposits, best marketing of financial products, best cheque clearance procedure, and best cartoon character for their bank ads.

Most popular by far was the money-counting competition – everyone's hands shot up for that. Kiyoshi, Michio and the others shouted so loud, in fact, that the classroom window cracked. In the end, the paper-scissors-stone method was used to choose the competitors, but when Kiyoshi and Michio lost, they stamped on the floor with such force in their frustration that they cracked one of the floorboards.

Kanae never raised her hand for any of the events, remaining cool and collected even when the money-counting competitors were being chosen. She kept scribbling furiously in her notebook, only now and then glancing up at the ruckus the boys were making.

'What's that you're writing?' I asked.

'My fantasy investment portfolio,' she answered.

Kanae had been building that portfolio since the third grade. At present, it amounted to a bit over thirty million yen on paper, though she had started it with a mere ten thousand yen in fictitious funds. She was pretty proud of that.

'So do you actually have thirty million in the bank now?' I asked in amazement.

She gave a derisive snort. 'I told you, it's a fantasy portfolio,' she said.

'Something like getting rich in The Game of Life?'

'A bit different. But not altogether.'

She turned away from me and back to her notebook. I noticed she had inserted earbuds in her ears. She was listening to the radio.

Sports Day was held in the autumn, and this time it was the grown-ups who won. They aced the money-counting, the best marketing of financial products, and almost all the other competitions. The kids were really disappointed. Only Romi Kawamata won anything, the runner-up prize for best cartoon character for her 'Sea Hare from Hell'. First prize went to the dog school principal, who of course had submitted a cartoon dog.

'That's so old,' the kids complained. 'Cartoon dogs haven't been cool for, like, ever.' But the judges were the bank's managers, so there was nothing anyone could do. Kanae didn't participate in the competitions, instead throwing her energies into the day trading of stocks, so that by the end she had raised her net worth past the fifty million yen mark. The cracks in the school window and floor were never repaired, standing as reminders of the local bank-run Sports Day, in which no event involved any form of physical activity.

Fruit

A princess moved into our neighbourhood.

'She's just an old lady,' snickered Michio and Kiyoshi Akai, but we girls knew better, so we decided to launch an investigation. The Princess lived on the north side of town in a cosy little bungalow, with Christmas roses in the garden and wild roses arching over the front door. The walls of the bungalow were painted light green, and the door was chocolate brown.

The princess worked in her garden in the morning, went to the local market at noon, and spent most afternoons sunning herself in the park, paying the occasional visit to the Love, where she and the owner would chat over a plate of heated-up pilaf from the freezer. She would return home before dark, close her lace curtains and turn on the light. She appeared to spend a full hour preparing dinner – partway through, a delicious smell wafted from the house. We could see her movements through the curtains. She would eat her dinner, clean up, and then sit in her rocking chair and read.

It took us a whole month to nail down this pattern. Since we were in school all day, we took turns feigning illness so that someone could always be tailing her.

'Just as I thought!' Kanae exclaimed. 'Only a princess would stick to a schedule this closely!'

For us girls, the princess was like a figure from a storybook. Raised by mice, wooed by a frog when she came of age, she ran away to escape him. Following many hardships, she met a prince and married. She left him in the end, and for the next fifty years lived a life of unrestricted freedom and luxury, then became an underworld figure, until, tiring of that one day, she suddenly dropped out of sight, taking pains to conceal her whereabouts. Word spread that she had died; yet now, after many years, she had come to our neighbourhood, far from the prince and the gangsters searching for her.

'Her life is perfect, don't you think?'

'Yeah. She even married a prince.'

'And made a pile of money.'

'And walked all over men, but they still followed her everywhere.'

'But isn't a princess supposed to be no bigger than your thumb?'

'They say it's cos she got as big as a regular human being after her wedding that she and the prince broke up.'

'No way,' Kanae's big sister put in. 'You mustn't believe in fairy tales,' she warned us. But none of us listened. We had other things on our minds. Like, how did one go about meeting a prince? Or ditching a frog? Or becoming an underworld figure? Beset by these hidden desires, we groped for some way – any way – to draw closer to the princess. Not one of us, however, was brave enough to approach her. So when the group of us came across Dolly Kawamata and the princess walking down the street talking quietly to each other, we lost our cool.

'Are those girls from around here?' the princess asked Dolly, referring to us. Dolly nodded in alarm. 'From what I've seen, children in this neighbourhood are hardly what one could call sophisticated,' the princess went on in a condescending tone. She shrugged at Dolly and walked off without so much as glancing at us. Only then did Dolly reveal that the princess had lived next door to her family during their stint in the United States. Night after night, Dolly told us, men driving Rolls Royces and Jaguars had visited the princess, the sound of popping champagne corks resounding beyond her walls.

'Tell us, Dolly,' Kanae asked, burning with curiosity. 'What were you and she talking about just now?'

'I asked her how to poison someone without being discovered.'

There was a persistent rumour, it seemed, that the princess had left no less than ten bodies buried in her back garden in America. But she had assured Dolly that she had gone straight and had no plans to murder anyone in our town.

'Is there anyone here that you would like to murder?'

Dolly laughed. 'Yes,' she said. 'Two people anyway.'

Many years later, when a mass murderer poisoned dozens of people across Japan, the princess was long dead and gone, but Dolly was in fine shape. Indeed, that was the year the branches of the fruit trees in the Kawamatas' back garden were so laden with fruit they almost touched the ground.

The White Dove

Kanae's big sister picked up something strange on her recent school trip.

It was not a major excursion. They didn't even have to board a bus: they just walked north-east to where the path to the top of Mount Golden begins and then up from there. The mountain is a mere 300 meters high. It took an hour to walk from the school to the start of the path, and another hour and a half to reach the summit.

Kanae's sister had no friends in the class. While all the other kids were doing stuff together – singing songs, getting scolded by the teacher for running around playing tag, giggling over shared secrets – she trudged glumly by herself at the back of the pack, eyes fixed on the ground.

'Come and walk with the rest of us,' Yamagami, the class representative, encouraged her over and over again (at the teacher's request), but she wouldn't budge. After seventeen tries, Yamagami finally gave up.

The fact was, Kanae's sister had experienced a prophetic dream the night before.

The dream had featured a little old woman and an old man ten times her size. The old man tried to crush the old woman underfoot, but she nimbly evaded him by leaping in the air time after time, until he fell on the ground in complete exhaustion. Without hesitating, she took a tiny, tiny needle and stabbed him in a vital spot, half killing him.

'Isn't marriage wonderful!' the old woman said. 'You can hurt each other like this any time you like!'

The old couple had celebrated their golden wedding anniversary long before and were well on their way to 'till death do us part'. Yet they never relaxed their guard, each waiting for the opportunity to deliver a fatal blow to the other. They appeared in Kanae's sister's dreams on a regular basis, about once a week.

A bubble emerged from the wounded old man's mouth. It was the size of a soap bubble at first, but it grew and grew until Kanae's sister could see herself inside. The view was hazy, but she glimpsed herself picking up a strange object from the mountain path she would climb the next day. That was why she had rebuffed Yamagami – if her classmates saw her, she would have to share whatever she found with them.

When they reached the summit, everyone pulled out their bento boxes. Kanae had played a nasty trick on her, though, just before she left the house that morning, secretly replacing the contents of her box – fried chicken, a small omelette and rice balls – with a mess of fermented soybeans. Kanae's sister had discovered this by the time she reached the corner of her street but she didn't care all that much – her sole concern was locating the strange object prophesied in her dream as quickly as possible. She left her class to their lunch and followed an animal track into the forest.

At a certain point the track came to an end. All was

dark. Then she saw a glow far ahead. A light seemed to be coming from a bamboo grove.

'What the hell?' Kanae's sister cursed. 'All this way to find Princess Kaguya, the Moon Maiden? Who needs that?'

Looking more closely, though, she realized that the light was coming not from the bamboo but from a long squishy plant shaped something like a garden hose. She ripped the plant off at the roots. What emerged from the stem resembled a white dove, and it smelled absolutely awful. Yet it wasn't a bird, or a god, or a goblin, just a very stinky *thing*. Kanae's sister pulled out her lunch box, scraped out the mess of fermented soybeans and replaced it with that malodorous whatever.

On the way back down the mountain, Kanae's sister's classmates gave her an even wider berth. She just smelled so bad. When she returned home and removed the lunch box lid, the stinky, dove-like *thing* flapped around her room. She knew that if Kanae discovered what she was keeping, she would get rid of it right off the bat, so she kept it in the box. It never left her side after that – it went with her to school and when she went out, and stayed with her when she was back in her room.

Slowly but surely, the strange white dove-like *thing* grew. When it had become too large for the lunch box, she let it roam free. It always came back at night, though, pecking at her window until she let it in.

The strange *thing* changed shape as it matured, going from white dove to something resembling a large green grasshopper, to, quite suddenly, something shaped like a human being. It still stank, but when Kanae's sister put clothes on it, it looked like a boy about her age.

Kanae's sister called the boy 'Grandpa'. Each day, she would call, 'Hey, Grandpa,' take a tiny, tiny needle, and run around him trying to prick him in a vital spot, often attacking from the rear.

The boy was fast on his feet, though, so she seldom succeeded. As he grew into a young man, it became even more difficult.

Raising the youth became a freer and easier matter when Kanae went off to study in France. Until then, Kanae's sister had kept him in the crawl space under the roof, but once Kanae's room was vacant, he stayed there, and they engaged in lavish amounts of sex all day long. Her parents were in the house, of course, but, unlike their children, they were an easygoing couple, so they never noticed the young man's presence.

The young man grew into his prime, and then into middle age. Kanae's sister entered her thirties.

'Hey, Grandpa,' she said one day. 'How about getting married?'

The middle-aged guy nodded. By that time, Kanae's sister was a celebrated *itako* medium on Mount Osore, the 'mountain of dread', speaking in the voices of the dead for those who came to communicate with them. They paid her well, so she was able to build a magnificent house for herself and her middle-aged husband at the foot of the mountain. He no longer stank; on the contrary, his sweet disposition made him popular with the young women who came to hear their dead relations speak through his wife's mouth, which led to numerous affairs. Kanae's sister knew about these, of course, but she left him alone – confronting him would have been a headache, and, besides, he wasn't a real person, just a strange *thing*.

When Kanae's sister was sixty years old, a huge meteor threatened the earth. Physicists had calculated its trajectory a year earlier and determined where it was going to hit. The place? Mount Golden, the exact same spot Kanae's sister had gone on her grade-school excursion.

Kanae's sister had another prophetic dream. In it, her middle-aged husband successfully turned away the falling meteor.

She asked him when she woke the next morning.

'I'm sad we have to part,' he said, wiping away a tear. 'But, yes, I will repel it for you.'

No sooner had he uttered these words than his shape reverted to that of a white dove. He flew higher and higher into the sky, growing ever more massive as he rose, so that when he met the meteor head on, the two dissolved in a great cloud, which drifted down to earth like snow.

Hailed as a hero, Kanae's sister was greeted with wild applause wherever she went, and statues of her were erected across the country. This had been her childhood dream, but when the statues actually went up, there was no joy in her heart. Instead, she spent her days quietly thinking, her mind on the strange *thing* that was no more. When it had abandoned human form and changed back to a white dove, its foul odour had returned as well. Till the day she died, Kanae's sister longed to smell that stench just one more time.

Eye Medicine

It was Dr Miranda of the Miranda Clinic who taught me that some people are hatched from eggs.

I know Miranda sounds like a foreign name, but it is actually Japanese. The weird combination of kanji made it look like it belonged to someone in a biker gang, though, so Dr Miranda decided to write it in katakana instead.

After working in a university hospital during his youth, Dr Miranda quit for personal reasons in his early forties and travelled the world for a number of years before returning to Japan in his fifties to open the Miranda Clinic. He rented a small seventy-year-old two-storey building on the outskirts of town, converted the ground floor into a clinic, and the upper floor into his residence.

Opinions about his abilities varied: some thought he was a fine doctor, while others dismissed him as a complete and utter quack. So while almost everyone in town knew about his clinic, those who used it were relatively few.

I went to the clinic whenever I had a cold, partly because it was seldom busy. Dr Miranda claimed to be able to handle all kinds of cases, so when a bug became lodged in my ear, I went there, and he extracted it without batting an eyelid. I had never seen a bug like it before.

'This species is peculiar to Central Africa,' he said, shaking his head. 'Where did you pick it up?' Of course I had no idea. After that Dr Miranda and I would sit and gossip when there were no patients around. He was an insect collector and was thrilled to add the bug he had taken from my ear to his collection.

It was during the rainy season when things were slow – patients suffering from allergies and the flu grew scarce then – that he told me about the egg people.

'There are quite a few around here,' he said, as if it were no big deal.

'How can you tell?'

'Medical training helps us recognize the signs, but the main thing is one's doctorly intuition.'

He confided to me that the dog school principal and Michio had hatched from eggs.

'But . . . how do you know?'

'Stop and think. Both of them are a bit different from the rest of us, wouldn't you say?'

I thought it over for a minute. But I still couldn't tell.

'So,' I went on, 'human beings born from eggs aren't really human?'

'Of course not. All mammals are viviparous.'

'Huh? You mean they're not even mammals?'

'Well, there are exceptions – take the duckbill platypus, for example – so I guess we could include them.'

Dr Miranda's tone had grown rather pompous. He whacked his belly like a sumo wrestler.

After that, I began paying more attention to the people in our neighbourhood. I roamed the streets studying their behaviour and their faces, their tendencies and their favourite foods, before coming to a decision about who had and who hadn't hatched from eggs.

After a while, it hit me that almost everyone had been hatched. Kanae and her sister, Kiyoshi, Dolly and Rumi, the lady who ran the Love, even my parents – they all had come from eggs.

The one exception was Dr Miranda.

'That's true,' he moaned. 'That's why I'm so lonely. Can you understand my loneliness?'

'No, I can't.'

'No, of course you can't.'

Cigarette smoke was billowing everywhere. The examination room stank of tobacco, and Dr Miranda's nurse poked her head in from the adjoining room to complain.

'See how my staff treats me? Is it any wonder I'm so lonely?'

'I see,' I answered. I found it difficult to sympathize with Dr Miranda, however lonely he might be.

Laying eggs was apparently a very pleasurable experience.

'When they lay their eggs, they secrete these special hormones, you know,' he explained.

Could I lay eggs at some point? I wondered. Dr Miranda glared at me for a second.

'Humans can't lay eggs,' he declared.

'Then you made it all up?'

'Nonsense. It just means that you are a real human being. Once in a blue moon a human is born into the world.

Then might I be as lonely as Dr Miranda? According to him, the best remedy for loneliness was an eye medicine made from a combination of antibiotics and boiled broccoli. A prescription was required for the antibiotics, but Dr Miranda said he could give me one whenever I needed it.

Weightlessness

For the first time in ages, we had a no-gravity alert.

'This is the Disaster Preparedness Office speaking. We have been informed that there is an eighty per cent chance that a no-gravity event will take place between two and five o'clock this afternoon. Please remain indoors during those hours. If you must go out for any reason, please make sure you are well weighted down. This has been a message from the Disaster Preparedness Office.'

This was broadcast three times during the morning on the loudspeakers positioned around our neighbourhood.

Our school day was brought to a sudden halt. We all gathered in the auditorium, where we were told to follow the evacuation procedures we had been drilled in, dividing into pre-assigned groups for the trip home.

Taking advantage of the fact that our group leader was a teacher new to his job, Kanae slipped away as soon as we were outside the school gate. 'C'mon,' she said, grabbing my hand. I had no choice but to follow her.

Kanae went first to the sandpit, where kids often played. No one was there. Then she went on to the vacant lot where we liked to hang out. No one there, either. Finally, she headed for the woods on the far side of the housing development.

'Let's go home,' I said, but Kanae just gave a contemptuous smirk and yanked my hand even harder. The big clock at the centre of the development already said past two. Suddenly I realized that I was indeed growing lighter. My feet were beginning to leave the ground, no matter how hard I waggled them to stay put.

'We'll be OK once we make it to the trees,' Kanae reassured me, quickening her pace. Hands clasped, we bounded along, rising higher into the air with each stride. Looking down made me woozy.

'You're making a big thing out of nothing,' Kanae scoffed. 'I mean, we're barely a metre off the ground.'

There were a number of other children in the forest but no familiar faces. Looking quite at home, Kanae latched on to a tree trunk and held her body upright, though it threatened to fly out in a diagonal or even horizontal direction.

'Ditch your backpack,' she ordered. I didn't want to at all – I was relying on it to give me at least some ballast. But she looked so scary I couldn't say no, so I bent over and slipped it off. It fluttered down to settle softly in the undergrowth.

I clung to a tree as my body grew lighter and lighter. Things began floating away: my backpack, dead leaves, a shoe someone had dropped, a handkerchief, a shopping bag. Everything that had fallen was now floating up to the sky.

'Oh, oh, look!' Kanae cried out in joy. Her voice sounded more child-like than I had ever heard it before.

Someone sneezed, which sent little balls of snot

wafting into the air. When I kicked my feet, my body strained to move forwards. We would have floated away had we let go of the trees, so we moved cautiously from trunk to trunk, like long-armed monkeys. Kanae managed to reach the far side of the woods.

'Hey, you guys!' someone called out behind me. I was so startled I almost lost my grip. Kiyoshi Akai had appeared out of nowhere. Right behind him, Kanae's big sister was glaring up at us with her usual baleful expression. Then, before we knew it, she was off, swinging from tree to tree, leaving only that baleful look behind.

'She's a real master at this,' Kiyoshi said in admiration.

The weightlessness lasted until late in the day, but when the sun began to set, gravity returned. Our bodies suddenly grew heavy, snapping the trunks of the more slender trees and sending the kids holding on to them tumbling to the ground. Backpacks, handkerchiefs, shopping bags, snot – it all came falling down. None of us got seriously hurt, though.

It was so much fun that we agreed with Kiyoshi that the more no-gravity alerts the better, but just then Kanae's big sister spoke from right behind my shoulder, as if she were glued to my back.

'Too much weightlessness causes osteoporosis, you know,' she whispered in a low voice, taking me by surprise.

Hair

After a hiatus of five years, a windstorm from the west-south-west deposited a huge pile of sand just outside our community. In response, it was decided that we would hold another Sand Festival.

Roughly a kilometre in diameter and ten metres tall, the pile was too soft to climb at first – the sand would suck you down – but efforts were made to harden it. After two weeks, it had been turned into a sand mountain, solid enough to walk upon. That allowed the town to run temporary power lines and water pipes to the top and erect a number of tents, a process that took another two weeks. When that was finally finished, people began to move in.

Traditionally, the Sand Festival is steeped in religion. But almost no one in our neighbourhood is devout. As a result, an occasional festival like this one becomes the focus for all kinds of beliefs. Grandpa Shadows predicted that a form of idol worship would be the most popular way to welcome the god, but his prognostications tend to be off, so people ignored him. The tent they flocked to after their midday nap was that of the old taxi driver who lived in the tenement. In the past, his forecasts had often hit the mark.

'I bet it'll be a bird god this time,' he said. 'The bird worshippers will rule the day.'

The tents could be used free of charge. Electricity was free too. The catch was that the power was shut off at 10 p.m., and didn't start up again until 6 p.m. the following day. There were people who stayed in their tents round the clock, waiting for the festival to begin, while others returned home at night to sleep. Outdoor stalls rose up around the tents. Once in a while, a handful of strangers would arrive from elsewhere after a week or more on the road, but they did their best to stay out of sight, slipping in and out of their tents as inconspicuously as possible. Their caution was understandable, for in the past there had been a brawl between outsiders and the people from my neighbourhood. The police had been called in, and a number of the combatants had to go to court. However, since all the jurors were people from my neighbourhood, the outsiders got the stiffest penalties, even though the locals were the instigators. The verdicts were appealed, of course, and the penalties reduced, but the legal process was expensive, and the outsiders ended up losing an awful lot of money.

Sure enough, one day the god made a sudden appearance at the festival, scattering virtue left and right from morning till night. The god left the following day, though, which meant people who hadn't been lucky enough to be there on that particular day totally missed out.

Every afternoon when school ended, Kanae, Kanae's big sister and I climbed the mountain. Though it was supposedly solid now, the edges were already eroding, which meant our trainers were full of sand by the time we reached the top. There seemed to be people everywhere. The tents were clustered at the top of the mountain. The throng surrounding the tent of the old taxi driver made it stand out, so the three of us decided to use it as our landmark, a base where we would meet before heading back home. That way we could roam freely without worrying about getting lost in the crowd.

On that day we all headed in different directions as usual. I was browsing through the stalls when something grabbed my ankle. A hand attached to a brown arm as knobbly as a wooden pole had darted out from the tangle of legs and feet to take hold of me. I kicked my leg like crazy to try and shake it off, but its grip was strong and I couldn't get away.

I stood there stock still, expecting the hand to release its hold eventually, but after five minutes its grip was as tight as ever. I was growing more and more afraid.

I was about to scream for help when a voice spoke to me inside my head. *Let it hang on*, it said. *If you put up with it, great good fortune will come your way.*

Great good fortune? The moment I heard that my greed took over. I knew I was in danger. But still I managed to stand there without moving, looking as nonchalant as I could, while evening turned into night. No one in the crowd paid any attention to me, and I was sure Kanae and her sister had already left, assuming that I had gone home first.

I remained there all night – the hand never released

its grip, not even when I got so tired that I sat down on the ground and nodded off.

When the sun came up the next morning, though, the arm suddenly vanished. At the same time a great bird came flying from the east. It was the sand god, no doubt about it. Once again, it scattered virtue on those gathered on the mountain before flying off at the stroke of noon. In years past, the god had hung around for the entire day, as it had on its first appearance this year, so those who missed it were left grumbling.

As soon as the festival was over, the sand mountain was demolished. I could hardly wait for my great good fortune to arrive, but so far nothing special has happened. The hand left a mark on my ankle, but now even that is gone. The knobbly arm does reappear from time to time when I am alone to gently cup my ankle in its hand. It does me no harm, though, and vanishes without a trace. I've even come to enjoy that feeling. But I doubt it can be called 'great good fortune'. The arm has no hair at all.

Baby

A new baby made its way to us, so we threw a big party to celebrate.

The baby came from the east. Three years had elapsed since it set out from a small country on the eastern frontier. It had been travelling all that time, passing through the necessary stages to become a fully fledged baby, until at last, on this very day, it arrived in our neighbourhood.

Three years ago, the baby had been a mere *fuyo*. A *fuyo* is about an inch thick and looks exactly like a book that can be held in one hand. The only differences are, first, that it can speak and, second, that it's soft to the touch. It has no arms or legs. It calls attention to itself by calling out. Amazed that a book can speak, someone will pick it up and then, repelled by how soft it is, hurl it across the room. If it lands properly, it changes form to become a *seto*.

A *seto* is a little person, a dwarf. (It can also be called *korobbokuru*, the Ainu word.) It only has one leg. Yet with that leg it can travel long distances. Being so small, it is naturally active at night. If it comes across a lost button on its nocturnal journey, it leaves it beside the pillow of its owner; if it encounters needlework left undone, it completes it overnight; if it finds a kitchen in disarray, it tidies it up by morning. A *seto* is thus a most considerate being.

However, a *mottsa*, the next stage of development, is a vile thing, the polar opposite of a *seto*. It too looks like a miniature person but is twice the *seto*'s height. They weigh about the same, though, which means the *mottsa* looks terribly emaciated. It has arms and legs like people do, but physical activity is not its strong suit, and there is a limit to how far it can walk. A *mottsa* will sneak into cars, trains and buses to get where it's going. It is hardly ever discovered, but if it is spotted, it verbally attacks, choosing the words it knows will wound its foe most severely and throw them into confusion. Some of its targets have even been known to die from those wounds. This is why you must never let a *mottsa* know that it has been seen. Instead, it is crucial to turn away as if you haven't noticed a thing. However, it often happens that the moment you encounter a *mottsa*, you let out an involuntary gasp. In that case, do not put on a tough front and pretend that its words do not hurt. The *mottsa* will just redouble its attack, saying even crueller things. Some people have lost control at this point, and have crushed the *mottsa* underfoot. A number of photos have been posted online of the bodies of a group of *mottsa* that were stomped flat on the floor of a bus one rainy day.

The next step in the making of a baby is the *hei*. The *hei* resembles a dinner plate. Since it has neither arms nor legs, nor the ability to make any kind of sound, it must wait in a pile for someone to come and move it. It seems that humans cannot resist the sight of a dozen *hei* stacked one on top of the other. They briskly wrap up the *hei* and cart them off to some distant place. When they get there, they remove the packaging and gently set the stack down on the ground. If there are less than a dozen, though, the *hei* look like grimy plates, nothing more. No one bothers to pick them up. As one can imagine, it's terribly hard for a *hei* to recruit enough comrades to make a full dozen.

When a dozen *hei* have been moved and laid on the ground, and night has fallen, they are transformed into *manemone*. *Manemone* are outwardly indistinguishable from human beings. Yet they speak only the language of dogs. Their intelligence is at the canine level as well. People tend to dislike them, for they often run with packs of dogs, or howl and mate with them. It is required that a *manemone* spend three days and nights with the dog who has become their soulmate before they move on to the next step in their transformation. This period is commonly spent in doghouses away from everyone else, but the fact that urban dogs now frequently sleep indoors has meant that, more and more often, a *manemone* has to try to sneak into someone's home unnoticed, which is next to impossible. Though some dog owners welcome a *manemone* to move in for those three days, this is extremely rare.

Once a *manemone* has spent the required time with its canine soulmate, it transforms into a *haro*. This is the final step in the making of a baby. A *haro* comes in the form of human twins. More specifically, it is a single entity divided into two halves. These pieces often become separated from one another, for the *haro* is a nervous creature, quickly distracted and prone to wandering off. If its two halves stray more than five hundred metres from each other, they vanish in an instant. It is said that the chances of a *fuyo* – the first step in the transformation process – making it all the way to *haro* is only about three per cent. Of that number, more than half separate and disappear.

This, then, is how the baby arrived in our neighbourhood. Who would take it home was determined by a lottery. It would never grow up, but would stay a baby. It would live, on average, eighty years. As a result, every one of us prayed not to be chosen. The draw was held at the celebration ceremony, right after the opening toast, and the winner was the old chicken farmer. Infuriated, he spent the rest of the ceremony cursing the outcome to anyone who would listen, but the baby innocently clung to him, and made no move to let go.

The Family Trade

Sōkichi Nashida had no desire to continue in the family business, so he left home after his high school graduation.

Sōkichi went to a distant town, found employment, enrolled in night school, and, after finishing there, landed a job as a stockbroker. He lacked any connections to the university old-boy network, which was a bit of a drawback, but he overcame that hardship to rise steadily in the company. Sōkichi's skill as a trader was immediately evident, but it turned out that he had a good feel for business as well, and he rose to the rank of Assistant Bureau Chief while still in his thirties.

That set Sōkichi Nashida to thinking. Perhaps it was time to chart a new course for his future. He was tired of moving large sums of money around on a daily basis, and the higher he rose, the more convoluted and unpleasant his relationships in the corporate world became.

So Sōkichi quit the brokerage. He had saved a pile of money, which he now used to support a life of travel. He stayed in the best hotels, and sought out the foods of the world in establishments ranging from Michelin three-star restaurants to roadside stalls. He dined on three-toed sloths, on ants. On badgers, giant arapaima and anaconda. On innards, brains and marrow. He suffered wrenching diarrhoea and raging fever. At such times Sōkichi Nashida retired to his bed, drank lots of water, and waited for his body to heal itself.

When Sōkichi Nashida tired of the gourmet life, he decided to get married. He would find a sweet, warm-hearted woman and they would work side by side in the fields, growing vegetables and a little rice, and keeping chickens and pigs. There would be snow in winter, wildflowers in the spring, chorusing cicadas in the summer, and bountiful harvests in the fall. To get things started, Sōkichi Nashida threw himself into the study of agriculture. He attended classes, engaged in fieldwork, established contact with a group researching new farming methods, until, in the twinkling of an eye, Sōkichi had become a central figure in the development of a large, cutting-edge agricultural enterprise. By establishing a cycle of farming that reduced chemicals and pesticides to a minimum and emphasized local production and consumption, he was able to revolutionize Japanese agriculture. Not only did this benefit the health of his fellow citizens, but Japan's economy took a turn for the better, and its relations with other Asian countries, the United States and the EU improved.

At this point, Sōkichi Nashida realized that he had totally deviated from his initial goal – finding a wife.

This set him to thinking again. He had taken a wrong turn somewhere. Immediately, he quit the farming movement and registered with a number of matrimonial agencies. Each week he was introduced to another 'perfect partner', and they would meet. Yet for some reason, none showed a willingness to embark on a wholly self-sufficient life with him. So Sōkichi Nashida set off on a walking tour that took him to farms around the country. Thanks to his connections in agriculture, he was warmly welcomed wherever he went. But the right woman never materialized. Some women admired the farming life and some women didn't, but neither type clicked with Sōkichi Nashida.

Sōkichi sensed that the problem might stem from some deficiency on his part, so he journeyed to Mount Koya, where he could live the life of a Buddhist ascetic. Once again, his powers of concentration stood him in good stead, for before long he had become a disciple of Mount Koya's most illustrious monk. The monk had four disciples in all, and together they were able to reform modern Buddhism, enlightening many of those who observed Buddhism only at funerals, and launching a broad campaign to convert non-believers. The number of pious Buddhists increased, in what amounted to a religious revolution. This too transformed Japan's relations with Europe, America, and the countries of Asia and the Middle East.

Once again, Sōkichi Nashida set to thinking. Was this not the perfect time to find a wife? He was now filled with virtue, and knew precisely how to control the bodily passions of the mundane world. For a second time, he registered with the matrimonial agencies and began meeting prospective partners on a weekly basis. All the women were smitten with Sōkichi. Sōkichi, however, had minimized his 'bodily passions' to such an extent that none of them aroused him in the slightest. He tried to convince them that, since he was already in his late forties, their marriage might be more of a tea-drinking relationship, but they all just shook their heads. 'A man is in his prime at your age,' they insisted.

Sōkichi Nashida thought some more. He decided to put the idea of marriage behind him. He had succeeded in his work. He had achieved enlightenment. Maybe it was time to go back home.

So Sōkichi returned to his hometown. The first person he went to see was the old chicken farmer. True to form, the old farmer went on and on, cursing his chickens and saying nasty things about people in the neighbourhood. Sōkichi also ran into Kanae, who dismissed him at a glance. 'What a middle-aged nerd!' she muttered. He spent three days and nights talking with Grandpa Shadows and the proprietress of the Love. Hachirō went around spreading the rumour that the three had once been schoolmates and had always been great pals, but, looking at them, it was hard to imagine that they were the same age. The Music House threw open its doors to Sōkichi Nashida, and he lived there for a year. It seems he intended to reinvent himself as a musician. But Sōkichi had no ear for music. So, for the last time, Sōkichi Nashida sat down to think about his future. There was no way around it. He had to go back to the family trade.

He came from a family of artists. Abstract artists, no less. Sōkichi Nashida disliked abstract art – in fact, there was nothing in the world that he hated more. But what could he do? In a feat of sheer self-discipline, he worked and worked, until in the end he had become a renowned abstract artist. If you leave Shibuya Station by the Hikarie exit, you will see one of his abstract murals on the corridor. He has founded a restaurant serving dishes of the most bizarre sort next door to his studio, and runs it pretty well. He remains unmarried.

The Bottomless Swamp

At long last, construction on the House of Sweets was complete. The scale far exceeded that of a house, though – in fact, the building was turned into a school, the School of Sweets no less.

The bulk of the school was made of chocolate. Dark chocolate, rich in cocoa. The surrounding fence consisted of ginger snaps. The roof was shortcrust pastry with an egg-yolk glaze that shimmered in the sun, while the light that passed through the hard candy windows sparkled. The walls and floors were a mosaic of cookies, and the railings were Mikado biscuit-sticks, baked especially big for the purpose. The blackboards were enormous Bourbon Alfort biscuits, topped with dark chocolate, while sweet pastries and salty rice crackers helped complete what was a highly detailed and intricate piece of architecture.

The weirdest parts of the school were the students' chairs, which were huge doughy dumplings, and the staff room, which was made of vegetable-based crackers and the like. The chairs were soft and comfortable – too comfortable perhaps: their one drawback was that those who sat in them quickly drifted off to sleep. The vegetarian staff room was supposed to promote the health of the teachers, but it was whispered that the real reason for it was that, at the neighbourhood association meeting, the old chicken farmer had loudly demanded the school buy his produce and wouldn't shut up until they agreed.

It was no easy task to pass the entrance exam to the School of Sweets. Not only were physical strength and mental ability required, so was luck and a nasty disposition. If an applicant lacked any of these, they would be rejected.

It was no surprise, then, that Kanae was the first from our neighbourhood to be accepted by the School of Sweets. In fact, she filled the requirements so perfectly that she didn't have to take the exam – instead, she was recommended by the selection committee. But Kanae never gave the offer a thought. The reason was that she had been a drinker since entering elementary school. 'They've got the wrong girl,' she spat on receiving the acceptance letter. 'You can't drink saké and eat sweets at the same time!' Then she tore the letter into small pieces.

Hachirō's older brother, Rokurō, went ballistic when he saw this, for he loved sweets more than anything in the world. He surreptitiously picked up the pieces and took them home, where he was able to reconstruct the acceptance letter well enough to manufacture a perfectly formatted counterfeit copy. Though furious with the insulting way Kanae had rejected the offer, Rokurō shrewdly turned that into an opportunity for himself. He became one of the first students of the School of Sweets, and was entrusted to deliver the speech at the school's opening ceremony on behalf of all students. 'Now I can eat sweets every day of the week. I'm one heck of a lucky guy,' was the gist of what he said. The principal looked a bit puzzled when he heard this, but his face was wreathed in smiles.

Of all the classes at the School of Sweets, home economics was the one that took up the most time. Daily cookery classes lasted more than two hours, while another hour was spent studying theory. Students were free to eat any part of the school they wanted at any time, but they had to repair and replace what they had consumed. If you had nibbled on a railing, for example, you had to bake a Mikado biscuit-stick just as big during your cookery period; if you had munched on a blackboard, you were obliged to create an identical Alfort biscuit.

It was relatively easy to replicate those parts of the school that were made of regular cookie dough or pastry, but brand names like Mikado and Alfort presented a problem, for it was hard to find all the ingredients listed on the packaging. At first, both principal and teachers insisted that students obtain each and every one of those ingredients, but as time passed, and students struggled to live up to this requirement, the rules were relaxed. When that happened, inevitably, the school's appearance began to change.

The result was the creation of a counterfeit school. As the building became less and less authentic – with counterfeit Koala Yummies, counterfeit Mikado biscuits, counterfeit chocolate-covered marshmallow Angel Pies, counterfeit Pringles, even counterfeit

Kabuki rice crackers – class attendance dwindled.

'The school's gone soft,' grumbled Rokurō. 'It's really pissing me off.'

'What can you expect – it's Rokurō,' sneered Kanae when she heard this. After all, he and his classmates were the only ones to blame for the flood of fakes that inundated their school.

In the end, the School of Sweets had to close its doors for good before the beginning of the summer holiday. Shrinking attendance was part of the reason, but the main problem was that the building was melting in the heat, turning into a bottomless swamp. Nor did anyone bother to demolish it. Summer passed, winter came, and the swamp froze hard as rock. Even now, whispered rumours that two students had drowned in the morass continue to circulate in our neighbourhood. Recently, Kanae's sister confided to me that Rokurō too was swallowed in the goo, and that the Rokurō we see today is himself a counterfeit, baked in the oven by his classmates during their home economics cookery class.

Falsification

It was Romi Kawamata who told me about the secret yet intense war that was being waged in our neighbourhood.

She began by mentioning the roof of the tax office.

'Did you notice that its colour and shape have changed?' she asked.

That place means nothing to me, so I just grunted, but she went on.

'And have you noticed that the door of the bakery that was on the right side is now on the left, or that it used to be automatic but now you have to push it open?' she asked, shooting me a quizzical look.

'You mean the place on the corner that sells sweet buns? That one?'

'Yeah, that one.'

According to Romi, lots of places in the neighbourhood were undergoing minor changes. Why was that happening?

'It's my sister Dolly's doing,' she said. 'One day she developed the ability to manipulate people's memories, and she's been using it ever since.'

If Dolly had set her heart on moving the bakery door from right to left, and the memories of everyone in the neighbourhood had been altered in that very second, then the door we had once remembered as being on the right was now perceived to be on the left. As a result, even though it was still actually on the right, we were swayed by our altered memory to see it as being on the left.

'Wow, that's really something! Is it connected to the intense war you mentioned?'

'You bet it is!'

Romi lowered her voice. Apparently, someone in our neighbourhood was highly sensitive to altered memory. Dolly's power had a limited effect on that individual, but the moment they saw the actual door, they knew something was off and their memory corrected itself within an hour.

'So they're the only one who can see the door as being on the right?'

'Yeah. And once that happens, everyone becomes able to see it. That single person is able to wipe out all the changes Dolly has accomplished – the whole metamorphosis of memory. It doesn't work anymore.'

Even the smallest hole is enough to send a balloon spiralling to the ground. The falsification of memory is like that. All it takes is one individual who remembers the truth, said Romi, for the whole edifice to collapse.

'That's why Dolly is waging a bitter war against that person,' she went on, lowering her voice to a whisper. 'That person', it turned out, was the woman who ran the Love.

The battle had already been going on for three months. Dolly's manipulations had started with the tax office roof and had gone on from there to include the home of the dog school principal, the bank, Prospect Park, and the speed of the river that ran between our town and the next. The principal's house had been moved from the heart of town to the top of a hill on the outskirts; the bank vault, which was previously underground, now sat, exposed, on the surface; a fleet of squid boats with dazzling lights had popped up around Prospect Park; and the river had turned into a raging, two-hundred-mile-an-hour torrent whose shores were now designated as unsafe to approach.

It wasn't only places – people had also been falsified. The changes were subtle but real. The dog school principal became the principal of a javelin training camp, Michio suddenly changed from a normal elementary-school student to the vice-president of the Chamber of Commerce, and the chicken farmer was turned from an old man into an old woman.

Quietly and imperceptibly, however, things began to return to normal, thanks to the efforts of the owner of the Love. The dog school principal abandoned his javelin throwers and was again surrounded by his dogs, large and small; the bank vault moved back underground; the squid boats disappeared; the river's current slowed; and Michio went back to being a student.

The effects of the falsification, however, remained. Grandpa Shadows's music box, which had been swept away by the raging river, never reappeared; the digestive system of Kiyoshi Akai's mother, who had fermented and eaten the squid her son had stolen from the squid boats, is still in wretched shape; and the mess that

Michio left at the Chamber of Commerce has yet to be straightened out.

When Dolly lost interest, the war finally came to an end.

'Tired?' Dolly is said to have asked the lady at the Love.

'Sure am. But I enjoyed the battle,' was the answer. Today, little is left of the falsification and its correction. The one exception is the old chicken farmer, who remains a woman. Her personality is the same as before, though, so everyone – even the two combatants, Dolly and the owner of the Love – has forgotten she was originally a man.

Refrigerator

The greeting squad swept into our neighbourhood this past autumn.

The greeting squad is comprised of five members. The first is the squad leader. Estimated age: mid-forties. Handsome face, slicked-down hair. Wears a suit most of the time. The next is his second-in-command. Female, early thirties. Bobbed hair, a long black apron over a tight skirt. The remaining members – male, female, male. They always walk three abreast, making it hard to get past them on the street. Despite the gender difference, their faces are impossible to tell apart. They may look in their teens, or in their fifties, or in their eighties, depending on the moment. The weather seems to be the determining factor. All three have bandages on their faces. The one on the right has a bandage on his right cheek, the one in the middle under her nose, the one on the left on his left cheek. The bandages are white and an inch square, and are plastered to their faces.

When the greeting squad spots someone from our neighbourhood walking alone, they waste no time in collaring them and launching into their litany of greetings. 'Good day,' the squad leader sings out. 'We bring you greetings of the day.' On cue, the members all bow politely and begin to introduce themselves.

'I am the leader.' 'I'm his second-in-command.' So far, so good. But the introductions of the other three are all over the place. I'm a sales rep. I'm a handyman's helper. I'm a housewife. I'm a moneylender. I'm a bird catcher. I fight for justice and truth. I'm a hunting dog. I'm a blue-ringed octopus. I'm Albert Einstein's great-grandson. I'm the Brazilian ambassador. There's no way in the world to know who they really are. To make things even more confusing, the self-introductions don't seem entirely random. The sales rep strikes one as a person engaged in sales. The Brazilian ambassador seems somehow ambassadorial. Blue-ringed octopus would seem one step too far, yet when they're introduced, the three junior greeters twine and twist together to create a distinctly octopus-like impression.

The continually shifting introductions of the line of three are not what make dealing with the greeting squad so difficult, however. No, the biggest nuisance is the fact that time grinds to a virtual halt while they are engaged in their routine.

It's not that time stops everywhere. It rolls along like normal for everyone else. But for those who are in the immediate vicinity of the greeting squad, it crawls at a snail's pace. It wouldn't be such a big deal if time stopped and then started again for the whole world – most likely no one would even notice – but it's a real drag when you alone are stuck in limbo like that.

When I bumped into the dog school principal the other day, he was still fuming about how the greeters had made him arrive too late at school to provide his own morning greeting to the staff. Even worse, after finishing their greeting, the greeters had suddenly begun to quarrel among themselves. The second-in-command accused the squad leader of eating all five of the doughnuts she had bought the day before, the line of three made some unwelcome cracks, and what had started as playful banter grew more and more heated until, finally, the left wing of the line of three pushed the leader to the ground and began to strangle him.

'So what happened then?' I asked. The dog school principal cleared his throat.

'The leader passed out,' he said, lowering his voice. 'Had to be carried off on a stretcher. A nasty business.'

I thought that incident would blow the greeting squad apart, but to my surprise the squad leader was out the next morning, fully recovered, his flattened hair in place.

'We come to offer you our greetings,' he said, smiling more brightly than ever, upon which all five began their round of introductions.

It struck me as strange that the five members could live this way, with no visible means of support, but it turned out they had opened a small French restaurant on the edge of town. Its name was the Konnichiwa, and it was a lot classier, and served much better food, than I would have expected.

Indeed, the Konnichiwa is thriving. Its customers come from far and wide, so many in fact that you have to book a table three months in advance. The food is exquisite, and the prices reasonable. The only possible drawbacks are that, first, the squad of five circulate from table to table greeting everyone, and, second, every so often they quarrel among themselves. When that happens, the customers pick up their plates and leave the restaurant, retreating to a spot where they can watch the fight. When it dies down, they carry their plates back to their tables and resume their dinner. Kanae told me that a greeter had been severely injured in one of those quarrels, and that they had locked him up in the refrigerator overnight. When he emerged the next morning, she said, he was as good as new.

The Shacks

It was Rokurō who discovered the cluster of four shacks just outside town.

'I bet there are ghosts inside,' he challenged the other boys. The mention of ghosts made it a test of courage. The boys got excited. Should they meet there after dark? Maybe try to catch some ghosts?

'Isn't summer the season for tests of courage?' someone asked.

'Not in modern society,' Rokurō declared pompously. 'These days, that stuff happens in early spring.'

It seems that the boys did trek out to the shacks that night, but no ghosts made an appearance, and it was so cold that a few days later Michio and Kiyoshi ran high fevers and had to miss school.

'See, the ghosts laid a curse on them!' Rokurō insisted, but by that time no one cared about the shacks any more.

It was thanks to Kanae's big sister that we learned the shacks were actually 'emotion rooms'. She had put the question directly to her class teacher, and he had explained that, of the four shacks, the pale red one was 'the sadness shack', the pale green one was 'the anger shack', the white one was 'the hate shack', and the yellow one was 'the shack of joy'.

Apparently, when anyone experiencing one of the

four emotions – sadness, anger, hate or joy – spent time inside the appropriate shack, it would expand, little by little, to cover more and more land. The shack would absorb human emotions and turn them into energy for its own growth. That was why gaps had been left between them – to give each shack room to grow.

Kanae and I went to check out the shacks one Sunday afternoon. We wanted to see with our own eyes how much they had grown after soaking up emotions for such a long time.

But the shacks were all so small and insignificant it was impossible to believe they had absorbed any emotions at all.

The following day Kanae went to confront her sister's class teacher after school.

'The issue is the degree of emotional purity,' Kanae reported him as saying. 'If you are filled with nothing but sadness, or hatred, then the shack will expand, but if your joy is mixed with sadness, let's say, or your anger contains even a shred of sympathy, then it won't grow at all. On the contrary, its walls and roof will start to crack.'

The teacher emphasized to Kanae the complexity of emotions, how impossible it was for any human being to feel hatred and only hatred, or anger and only anger. Such a person could not exist, he concluded with a smirk.

'What a creep. I can't stand him!' Kanae said with a frown. Then a wave of relief crossed her face. 'Ah,' she exclaimed. 'This is pure anger! Let's head for the shacks!'

Kanae grabbed my hand and we ran and ran until we were standing before the light green shack. Inside, the light was dim and the air chilly.

'You have to wait outside', she said, shoving me out and closing the door. After about five minutes, the shack began to swell until, almost before I knew it, it was bulging against the white shack next door. I thought that would be the end of it, but then it began to shoot up in the air. Two, three, then four storeys, with a big balcony jutting out from each floor. As I watched, it grew and grew, until it had reached Tower of Babel proportions.

When the sun began to go down, Kanae finally emerged from the shack, looking completely refreshed. 'That guy really pissed me off,' she said, squinting up at what had been created by the energy her anger had unleashed.

News of the tower spread quickly, so that by the next morning people from our neighbourhood were eagerly cramming themselves into the small shacks. Not one of them, though, possessed Kanae's pure emotion, so the shacks did not expand. Instead, their walls sprouted cracks, and their roofs began to tilt. Only Kanae's 'shack of anger' was able to maintain its shape, but by afternoon even that towering edifice had collapsed, scattering pieces of its skeleton across the site.

The shacks still sit at the edge of town, but almost no one dares to go inside. The exception is the dog school principal, who uses them to train his dogs. They romp into the 'shack of joy', barking away. By now, at least a hundred dogs have played in there, wagging their tails and jumping for joy; yet the shack is hardly any bigger, covering only a square metre.

'In the end, a dog is just a dog,' Kanae likes to brag. Nevertheless, not a single crack mars the walls of 'the shack of joy'. There can be no doubt – dogs' emotions are pure too.

The Empress

Once again, our shopping arcade held its annual lottery. Shoppers receive one ticket for every five hundred yen they spend, with ten tickets required to take a shot at the draw. The prizes are always the same: fifth prize is a small packet of tissues; fourth prize a bottle of cooking oil; third prize a voucher for a thousand yen's worth of free merchandise from the arcade's shops; second prize a box of mandarin oranges; and first prize is three wishes.

The year before last, the first prize went to a bachelor who had just moved into the neighbourhood. That caused quite a commotion, for the simple reason that he didn't have a clue what he was doing. The result was that, as might be expected, he made the same sort of stupid mistakes you see in fairy tales. His first wish was for the most beautiful woman in the world. A second later and, *voilà*, there she was in his tiny bachelor pad. When he made the wish, the young man was blissfully unaware of the troubles involved in living with the world's most beautiful woman. But he soon found out. Her great beauty caused him equally great hardship: she spent money like water, complained no end about their poverty, and went into hysterics if he so much as thought about anything but her. This led the man to make his second wish: that she turn into the world's most submissive and obedient woman. Again, the change was instantaneous. However, the woman submitted not just to him but to all men. The world's most beautiful woman was also the most pliant, willing to hop into bed with any man who propositioned her. You can easily imagine the impact on our neighbourhood of having the world's most beautiful and most submissive woman living in our midst. Public morals went out the window to such an extent that, at one point, the elementary school had to suspend classes.

'The stuff grown-ups do to each other is amazing!' said Kiyoshi and Michio, barely able to contain their excitement after peeking through windows at the goings-on. The neighbourhood women, however, stood back and coolly recorded every word their menfolk uttered. You can easily imagine the panic of the men, once the commotion had subsided, when those words were thrown back in their faces. In the days that followed, women were able to exert complete control. Good luck to any man who tried to complain, too, for a record, including visual evidence, was made available at the town hall, where a large screen exposed male malfeasance on an endless loop.

What could he do? The man used his third wish to wish away the world's most beautiful, most submissive woman. At first, the men in our neighbourhood lamented her sudden disappearance, but they soon calmed down. In fact, they seemed to have already forgotten how crazily they had behaved with her. Kanae and I, though, felt pity for the way the most beautiful woman in the world had been so wholly forgotten, so we got together to say prayers for her from time to time, a custom we continue to this day.

Last year, the first prize was won by Hachirō's father. His three wishes were all for money. Since payouts were capped at a million yen each, not many winners asked for money, but his family was so poor that it made a real difference. In fact, he asked for the whole amount in cash right there on the spot. People found the decisiveness with which he made this request so refreshing that they awarded him the title of Father of the Year, which carried a prize of an extra hundred thousand yen. Thanks to this sudden influx of money, the Hachirō lottery was suspended for six months, and Hachirō went back to living with his family instead of rotating from house to house.

He had been away from home a long time, though, so the new arrangement didn't suit him. 'I can't handle this,' he complained to anyone who would listen. 'I mean, everyone there has the same genes as me!'

This year the draw was won by the lady who runs the Love. Usually, people were able to guess what the winner's three wishes would be, but in her case none of us had a clue.

'Maybe she'll wish for a better menu for the Love,' Kanae said. I was surprised – I thought that was a pretty lame guess, not up to Kanae's standard at all. She ruefully admitted that she had batted the question around in her mind, twisting and turning it every which way, only to settle on that boring answer.

I guessed that the woman who runs the Love would wish for a perfect score on her karaoke rendition of 'Hardly Worth Confessing', but Kanae and her sister gave that the thumbs down. No one would waste a wish on anything so petty, they said.

Of the three of us, Kanae's sister's choice of 'world domination' sounded the best, though it was something anyone in town could have thought up.

In the end, though, 'world domination' turned out to be the Love owner's actual wish, for, not long afterwards, her face was transformed into that of an empress. The world started getting along better, and peace reigned. I could have done without the strains of 'White Butterfly Samba' blaring from loudspeakers around the globe every morning and night, but, as Kanae's sister kept lecturing me, that was a small price to pay for world peace, so I held my tongue.